Imagining Personal Data

T0386177

Imagining Personal Data

Experiences of Self-Tracking

Vaike Fors, Sarah Pink, Martin Berg
and Tom O'Dell

Routledge
Taylor & Francis Group
LONDON AND NEW YORK

First published 2020 by Bloomsbury Academic

Published 2020 by Routledge
2 Park Square, Milton Park, Abingdon, Oxon OX14 4RN
605 Third Avenue, New York, NY 10017

Routledge is an imprint of the Taylor & Francis Group, an informa business

First issued in paperback 2021

A catalogue record for this book is available from the British Library.

A catalog record for this book is available from the Library of Congress.

ISBN13: 978-1-350-05138-6 (hbk)
ISBN13: 978-1-03-208207-3 (pbk)

Typeset by Integra Software Services Pvt Ltd.

Contents

List of Figures

Acknowledgements

This book is the outcome of collective research in which all four authors participated, playing out particular roles in relation to our different research interests and expertise. Without this collaboration the book that has resulted would have been impossible for any of us as a sole author endeavour, and we are grateful to each other, the Swedish Foundation for Humanities and Social Sciences (Riksbankens Jubileumsfond),[1] who funded our research, and to our respective universities for the opportunity and support they provided. We similarly thank the many people who have supported our project as research participants, giving us their valuable time to discuss and show their uses of self-tracking technologies and personal data. We have represented those who chose this option with their first names in this book, others have pseudonyms according to their wishes and our research ethics. Without their enthusiasm for our project, likewise this book would have been impossible.

While we are the authors of the text presented here we also acknowledge the contributions that others have made to our research and thinking. We would like to thank Shanti Sumartojo, who undertook fieldwork discussed in Chapter 5, within a cycling and self-tracking study undertaken collaboratively with Sarah Pink, Deborah Lupton and Christine Heyes LaBond. Deborah Lupton also gave valuable input to the conclusions in the same chapter. We also thank participants in the Data Ethnographies workshop series, based at RMIT University while Sarah Pink worked there, particularly Robert Willim, Melisa Duque, Débora Lanzeni, Elisenda Ardèvol and Francesco Lapenta, who participated in our Broken Data workshop. We also had valuable discussions of our research with our colleagues within the international *Self-tracking and automatised bodies* network, funded by the Swedish Foundation for Humanities and Social Sciences, and led by Martin Berg, in particular Deborah Lupton, Minna Ruckenstein and Mika Pantzar. A special thanks goes to Minna Ruckenstein, who has been very helpful in discussions about the foundations and futures of the Quantified Self community and other similar phenomena, and for putting us in contact with one of the leading figures of the Finnish BioHacker community, Teemu Arina. Jonnie Eriksson helped us to clarify philosophical underpinnings of biohacking and the traces of transhumanism in contemporary self-tracking practices.

We also want to thank Thomas Blomseth Christiansen, Jakob Eg Larsen and Sara Riggare, who generously shared their thoughts about the future of self-tracking, based on their own extensive self-tracking experiences, their long-term engagement in the Quantified Self community and their own academic research. Likewise we thank Kourosh Kalantar-Zadeh and Chris Dancy for taking the time to discuss their individual projects with us. We also received inspiring input from the Future Self-Tracking workshop we organized at Halmstad University on 24 November 2017. This interdisciplinary workshop with researchers, developers and designers was facilitated by Pontus Wärneståhl, and Thomas Blomseth Christiansen, Jakob Eg Larsen, Kalle Jonasson, Susanne Lindberg, Thomas Lindgren, Jesper Lund, Lina Lundgren, Jens Lundström, Carljohan Orre, Wagner Ourique de Morais, Anita Sant'Anna and Rachel Charlotte Smith were invited participants.

Prologue

Confessions of a novice self-tracking research team

The production of personal data through digital self-tracking involves people using and engaging creatively and analytically with wearable, digital, mobile and locative sensor and computing technologies to record data and quantify and analyse various aspects of human activity. This includes walking, running, cycling and other forms of movement, heart rate, sleep, calorie intake and expenditure, stress levels and much more. The origins of the rise of digital self-tracking lie in the commitment to the measurement, monitoring and sharing of personal data in self-experimenting communities that indulge in technology-oriented do-it-yourself biology, such as biohackers and the Quantified Self members. In recent years self-tracking has become ubiquitous in everyday life contexts as well as being tested and used – to varying degrees of success – in wider settings, for example, health, educational programmes, efficiency management in work life, in the management of personal relationships, in postnatal care, and in caring for and tracking the movements of pets.

But what happens in the wake of the hype, when ordinary people take on the project of digital self-tracking in their everyday lives? How do their uses, expectations and imaginaries relate to the history of self-tracking, to the ideas that underpin the development and design of contemporary self-tracking devices and apps, and to how early adopters in self-tracking communities and top-end researchers imagine future self-tracking?

As Teemu Arina, a leading figure in the Finnish biohacking community, said regarding self-tracking in the context of biohacking at the 2015 Biohacker Summit in Helsinki:

You might have a hypothesis – if I do that, that will happen. But you don't
know until you try. I might have a scientific understanding of it, in research
papers they might ask different kind of experts, but really you don't know
until you test. (Arina, quoted in Berg, Fors and Eriksson 2016: 115)

Our work as researchers is always inflected by our own personal lives, and in
the following chapters we examine the personal as it intersects with data and
technology. As we started our research we realized that we likewise needed
to know more about how personal data felt, and what it would feel like when
it was no longer so personal but was shared with others. In this prologue,
we ask: what could a group of researchers learn and know about themselves
by collectively using self-tracking devices in their ordinary everyday lives?
And what might readers want to know about them before considering their
interpretation of how other people live and imagine their futures with data?

We developed an auto-ethnography experiment, in which all four of
us donned a Jawbone UP wearable wristband and logged into the Jawbone
companion app on our smartphones to track and share with each other our
sleep and exercise data over a period of a few months, and across the world
between Sweden and Australia. We had been working together for several
years and already knew that we had quite different experiences of self-tracking,
exercise and everyday dietary preferences. Using this wearable device, with
all its promises about guiding us towards a better life by producing and
deciphering personal data, we all looked forward to embarking on a journey
in which, as Tom put it when deciding on which device to use, 'I'm sure we'll
learn more about each other than we ever thought we wanted to know.'

We learned about how our lives could be condensed into data, the
implications of this for our real-life experience of our activities and how we
had imagined that the self-tracking would be part of our lives, and how little
both our own and other people's data could really tell us about what people did
in their lives. We also learned about some of the underpinning principles that
would recur as our research unfolded throughout our investigations of other
people's experiences of self-tracking technologies and data. It was from the
outset of this collective self-tracking experiment that the themes of this book
began to germinate as our auto-ethnographic experiences drew our attentions
to the sensoriality, spatiality, technological possibility and human improvisation
that our uses and experiences of self-tracking technologies and personal data

entailed. That is, through thinking about our personal experiences as starting points for our work, or connecting back to them once other participants' experiences began to resonate with ours and invoke memories of them, the correspondences between the personal and the patterns through which the everyday emerges began to surface. As scholars from different disciplines – anthropology, pedagogy, sociology and ethnology – we were each attentive to experiences that resonated with our own practice and theory. Bringing these together created a site where our experiences of sharing our use of the same technology within different lives could intersect in ways that brought together the personal and scholarly.

Sarah is a design anthropologist who incorporates exercise into her everyday life by walking and sometimes cycling, but infrequently exercises for the sake of exercising and never participates in competitive sports. Her interest in exercise is in how it can become part of life, in ways that are collaborative and useful rather than being competitive or being an obligation towards staying healthy. Having already used a smartphone self-tracking app – Moves – for a few months, she looked forward to using the Jawbone wristband and app to gain a deeper understanding of how much exercise she actually did and of her sleep patterns. During most of the time she used the wristband and its own app she continued to use the Moves app. Each app tracked differently and, she was not surprised to discover, gave different readings of her daily steps. In this sense, from early on Sarah was not particularly interested in the idea of the apps providing her with accurate readings of her activity, as much as offering an estimation of what she might have done, and how this compared to the distance, steps or other activity she might have covered or engaged in on previous days. In short, she was already prepared for the reality, which is advanced in critical data studies, that personal data is not truthful, objective or complete. Given that her previous way of knowing how much exercise she had done was based on extremely rough estimates or knowledge of, for example, the distance she would have to walk to work, she saw the data as new – albeit uncertain and not all that reliable – knowledge and was in fact elated that she appeared to be exercising far more than she had ever imagined. As we discuss in the following chapters, the idea that the use of self-tracking technologies will 'improve' our behaviour, by amongst other things increasing the amount we exercise, has been part of their hype. Yet in Sarah's case the apps failed to encourage her to exercise more, and instead comforted her that she was already exercising sufficiently by integrating walking and cycling activity into her everyday life. Like other participants in this project, Sarah did not change her behaviour to suit the apps but, rather, used the technologies in ways that were meaningful for the life she already led.

However, during this time, both Sarah's everyday life and functionality of her technology were quite changeable, which was another factor that contributed to her not using the apps consistently. She often travelled overseas to go to conferences and participate in projects, and she was not always very vigilant of the needs of the technology. As a result there became a series of gaps in Sarah's self-tracking data, usually caused by her forgetting to charge her smartphone, going overseas and changing her SIM and data plan, and a smartphone software update after which the wearable and smartphone could not connect. As a result her data trace became broken in various places, which led her to the concept of 'broken data' (Pink et al. 2018). Sarah's own experiences connected to her research interests in how people improvise with technologies and data and how this is framed through the contingent circumstances of their everyday lives. This design anthropological theme, which we explain further in Chapter 2, helps us to consider how technologies become part of human lives, imaginations and futures rather than seeing human lives and society as a whole as being impacted on by new technologies, as is so often assumed.

Eventually Sarah, like many users of body-monitoring technologies, as discussed later in this book, 'gave up' purposefully self-tracking. The demands of Jawbone to engage with the app and register changes in activity were not realistic for her schedule or all that interesting to her, and the Moves app used up too much battery time on her smartphone. Yet the experiment had opened her towards thinking in new ways about her physical activity and offered alternative modes of measuring – albeit inaccurately – and knowing health-related aspects of her life. At some point – she cannot remember when – she realized that in fact the free Apple Health app which was already installed on all iPhones was already tracking her steps, and offered her an alternative 'background' mode which she could dip into when she wished. This could mean not opening the app for months, but sometimes circumstances configured to draw the data into new modes of learning about, knowing and imagining aspects of her life. When Sarah spent two months as a Guest Professor in Denmark in 2018 she used the app to understand how she moved around her new city, usually on foot, the steps she had taken and the distances she had covered. Suddenly the app started to have meaning as she sought to situate herself and her activity in a new environment, of which digital technology and data were inevitably a part, and checking the app became part of a familiar everyday routine of smartphone use. Yet once she returned to Melbourne she soon forgot to check the app, except for the occasional look when she wondered if she had walked an exceptional distance or had a moment free on the tram or before going to sleep. These questions of learning, meaning and environment resonate through this book. As human futures continue to develop with technologies and data, as an integral part of the worlds they emerge in, how do we imagine our futures with personal data? For some of us it seems to have become a part of the world, something in the background that we can dip into and that has become so familiar that it seems inane, benign and simply ordinary. Can we even imagine our lives without personal data? Yet as we move into a complex technological era, sometimes called the fourth industrial revolution, there are wider issues and questions about the safety, power and politics of our data and how it is accessed and shared. What anxieties do we need to navigate? Where should we be cautious and protective? And do we even have the power to do so?

Vaike's physical exercises are connected to being an active horseback rider, and she spends time at the stables at least three times a week. In between these activities she prefers to do her physical exercise by having an active life and likes to spend time outdoors in nature. She has not been competing in sports for the last twenty years or so, but wishes that she had more time to do sports with friends. Due to a bad back she is compelled to do gym training, which she finds boring. Therefore, she never keeps to regular gym training for more than two months in a row (but she always starts all over again six months later with high expectations). She hoped that using the Jawbone UP actually would give her the push to regularly train, as promised in the marketing, but she would never have tried it if it wasn't for the fact that she would do it together with the other three people in the research group. She had read recent studies that showed that the average American would use this kind of app on average for three months before it would end up somewhere useless in the home, and she became curious about two things: why do people tend to stop using it after a couple of months, and which, if any, of the produced visualizations and data points would she find the most interesting to have a look at. Shortly after starting to use the Jawbone, she noticed that the one graph that really caught her interest was the sleep tracking, and after a while it turned out that her initial question, why people tend to stop using self-tracking apps, might be a question of how the app fits into what people already knew and did, and how it opened up new possibilities to learn more about what they, in an embodied and unspoken way, already knew. Soon enough, the sleep tracking became part of her daily routine, activating it before she went to sleep became part of the routine of putting her alarm on and hooking up her phone with the charger, and checking the sleep data became part of shutting the alarm off in the morning, feeling through how her back felt and if she had one of her recurring morning headaches or not.

However, this was not the primary reason why she got caught by the sleep-tracking feature. It was basically the fun-factor that made her open the graph to see how her sleep had been visualized by the app. Not for any particular reason, just for the fun of looking at how the rest of the group had slept the previous night, she found it interesting to 'check-in' the sleep status of the group every morning. Even though she could not see how well they had been sleeping in qualitative terms, more when they went to sleep, woke up and if they had to get up and do something in the middle of the night, this was a new route to communicate with the others. However, the novelty of this feature faded rather quickly and after a while she concentrated more on understanding her own sleep, or rather she tried to figure out how the data correlated to what she in some ways already knew. This correlating practice, to merge the embodied and the visualized 'data-sets' and see how well the datafied world 'understood' her life, continued for a couple of weeks until she got tired of the fact that it didn't give her any new sensations or insights that she could bring with her in her pursuit of dealing with everyday life. When she started to search for other people's experience of this disjuncture between their experience and how it was visualized in the app, she found numerous blog posts discussing this topic. One example is Carolyn Thomas (2014), who blogged about how she couldn't see that her Fitbit tracker gave her any relevant information in addition to what she already knew. By comparing her own account of her Saturday morning with the data produced by her Fitbit during the same period of time, she came to the following conclusion:

> Will knowing what my Saturday morning looks like on a Fitbit graph change at all what I do or how I do it on Saturdays? Will I now start jogging through the farmers' market to try to boost that moderate intensity walk up to high intensity? Will I stop buying all those heavy veggies that seem to slow me down on the walk home? No. No. And no.

This example sheds light on the disjuncture between the designed data-world produced by a Fitbit and the lived experience of the performed activities that become too big to be reconciled by the user. The problem seems to be that the self-tracking technologies often rest on the idea of the possibility they offer of providing precise metrics and accurate facts about the user's body and that this information in a straightforward manner could be transferred into knowledge about the user that helps them to transform their lifestyle and behaviour. If you then treat the data that is produced as such you will inevitably be disappointed. The personal data does not provide *new* knowledge, it is already part of what you in a sensory, unspoken and embodied way already know after being engaged in the measured activities. Furthermore, self-tracking cannot be seen as something extra beyond the daily routine, it is through the routine that it becomes connected to everyday life and thereby becomes possible to add something meaningful into it. When starting to think differently about the purpose of self-tracking data and what it could add to the lived experience of the measured activities, Vaike started to look for other ways of using the apps than the intended. This relationship with how data is imagined and how it can become part everyday life is central to this book. Opening up for new perspectives on self-tracking – beyond the intended use and design imaginaries – also opens up for a broader understanding of what it can do in everyday life.

Vaike stopped using her Jawbone wristband when she lost two parts of it. Firstly, the small cap that covered the charging plug on the wristband disappeared. This quickly became an annoying everyday problem since the plug kept on getting entangled in materials in the environment, such as clothes, bags and other things that came too close. Secondly, she also lost the small charger for the wristband, and by that time she was so fed up with having to adjust to wearing the wristband that got stuck everywhere that she put it in a drawer and left it there. Fast-forwarding to 10 December 2018, Vaike has used a sleep tracking app for 463 days in a row, not so much because she really needs to, or is particularly interested, any longer, but just because it has become part of her morning and evening routines. She is also having fun tracking her walks and riding tours in an app that allows group challenges. The way she tries different apps, ditching some and embedding others in everyday routines, is not based on imaginings of what she might *know about* her activities through self-tracking technologies but instead on paying attention to what she might *learn with* them. This approach is key in the book and opens up self-tracking as much more than a tool for superficial kinds of behavioural change.

Martin is a sociologist with a history of yo-yo dieting and irregular workouts as long as his not always overused gym membership. Often he finds it easier to plan for future workouts and diets rather than actually hitting the gym and making proper meal preparations. Sometimes fairly fit, other times not so fit, Martin has used different kinds of self-tracking devices over the years, mostly in order to increase his fitness level or to lose some or many extra pounds when needed. Calories, steps, running distances and sleep patterns have been tracked both using self-constructed spreadsheets and more technically advanced wearable devices and connected scales. What all these ways of tracking had in common was that they didn't provide any particular feedback on the recorded data. Instead, it was always up to him to find out whether any change had taken place or if there were any particularly interesting correlations between different data points, such as for instance weight measurements and steps taken. This meant that the practice of self-tracking was largely a question of recording data automatically, whereas the actual analysis of those data had to be done by himself – something that had failed many times, at least when such an analysis was supposed to be transformed into action (i.e. actually continuing going to the gym and maintaining a healthy and balanced diet). The Jawbone UP 'Smart Coach' system promised that there would be a 'better version' of himself out there and he was keen on getting to know that other version of himself. For this reason, he decided, as part of our collective auto-ethnographic experiment, to slavishly (at least that was the initial plan) follow the advice of his wristband and companion app in his journey towards what was said to be his better self. In his field notes from the experiment the following was jotted down on the first day of his journey:

On a cold Sunday evening in February 2015, I went to my local Apple Store to purchase a brand new Jawbone UP 24 wristband. I recall being very excited and attracted by the thought of wearing a machine that would tell me, as it promised, how to become a better person. The wristband was marketed with the words 'There's a better version of you out there, get UP and find it!' Despite my immediate curiosity I was confused. How was I supposed to find a better version of myself? Who could the better me possibly be? Would I enjoy that version more than the current? I unwrapped the packages, put on the wristband and downloaded the companion app. The app requested me to enter some basic bodily stats such as age, weight, height and so on and, once entered, they were quickly transformed into recommendations on objectives. Not very surprisingly, the app suggested that I should lose weight and gave a general recommendation to walk at least 10,000 steps a day and sleep for 8 hours per night. There was nothing special to these objectives but I couldn't stop thinking about how they related to the transformation into a better version of me. Somehow, I felt like an old car going for an annual service.

Despite the promises of advanced data crunching to gain an understanding of the complexities of one's everyday life, the device forced him to understand his body and self with and through a language that was lacking context and nuances. In most cases, physical activity was simply measured using steps as a form of communicative currency which means that, to take one example, all walks are thought of as having a similar meaning. By using steps as a measurement, nothing is said if the walk is taken among beautiful autumn leaves in Seoul, Korea, or when trying to find a good chilled lager somewhere in a sweaty Sydney. It might be that the apps applaud the user for having walked the suggested daily 10,000 steps, but they can't see the qualitative difference from when the same amount of energy and time is spent running between the printer, the coffee machine and the desk at the university department. Instead, all kinds of activities are measured and communicated through the perspective of the app and then communicated with a language that is somehow easily quantifiable. Yet, the lack of complexity allows for physical activity and indeed inactivity to become something that can easily be reflected upon, talked about, compared and experienced in ways that weren't possible before. The data allowed us to reflect on personal pasts by reading distances walked and nights slept. But the very simplistic and problematic way of presenting data made experiences of physical activity mediated in ways that were both comforting and annoying. The wristband sometimes felt like a little toe: completely useless yet very important for keeping balance. But at the same time it was a balance that needed the user's imagination to become contextualized. The tension between being useless and promising, as Martin imagined this self-tracking device, led him to investigate further how technologies of this kind are presented and discussed, by designers and in promotional materials, *as* meaningful. It seemed to be the case that devices and apps of this kind need the body and the world in which it is situated to be imagined in a certain way in order for them to become meaningful and to make sense as contexts for self-tracking. Martin soon noticed that several self-tracking technologies tend to assume that people are in need of assistance and guidance since they are believed to find it difficult to understand what is best for their lives and body. At the same time, however, they are imagined as technologies that can empower users and help them take control of their lives. These tensions between what self-tracking technologies do – and can do – in relation to how they rely on certain assumptions of people, their bodies and everyday lives, have become a key theme for this book, running through historical accounts of self-tracking as well as more contemporary and design-oriented ones. The promises of such technologies, and the problems that might arise when they cannot account for the complexity of human bodies and the contingencies of everyday life, could well be one explanation as to why people tend to ditch or simply forget about their self-tracking devices after a while. Or, to continue buying new self-tracking devices in the pursuit of a life that is happier and healthier, thus leaving old and sometimes broken devices in device graveyards, such as the ones shown in Figure 0.1.

Tom trains on a daily basis, 75–90 minutes in the early morning, working out in the gym every other weekday, and running or biking the other weekdays, running on average 10 kilometres per pass. He reserves longer runs and biking sessions for the weekend. He trains in martial arts four evenings a week (2 hours per pass) and has a black belt in kobujutsu and iaido, and a fifth dan black belt in jujutsu. He looked forward to using the Jawbone and wondered what it could teach him about himself. During the spring of 2015 when Tom was participating in our collective self-tracking experiment, he noticed that

Figure 0.1 An Apple Watch, a Fitbit, a Withings Pulse, a Jawbone UP wristband and some random accessories. Photo: Martin Berg.

it included a sleep-measuring function in the Jawbone UP system which he never understood. He found that the mornings he felt most well rested, the Jawbone told him he had not had much deep sleep, and on the mornings he felt exhausted, the device told him he had a wonderful night of deep sleep. No matter how fast or slowly he ran, it always reported the same average time for his running but could report a discrepancy of up to a half kilometre in the distance he ran, even if he ran the exact same route day after day. But, throughout the experiment, he kept looking at the graphs the App produced and comparing himself with the teammates. His own impression of the Jawbone, however, fell in line with a review he read online on 'The Buyer's Guide: Jawbone Up24' (n.d.) by a man who calls himself 'Justjeepin'. On 16 April 2015, Justjeepin wrote:

> I loved the idle alert and the ease of switching modes to sleep and back and the feel of the band better than my wife's Fitbit Flex BUT I returned the Up24 because it wasn't correctly counting steps. There were many times it wouldn't count steps at all and other times it was off by a large amount.

I tried another Up24 in hopes that my first was defective but it still wasn't counting steps correctly.

The Jawbone was a slick, easy to use and comfortable monitoring device that quantified Justjeepin's daily life. But Justjeepin couldn't really recognize the reflection he saw in the numbers the Jawbone provided him. Who was looking back at him in the mirror? What was distorted, the Jawbone's reflection or Justjeepin's perceptions of himself? What Justjeepin was looking at, and what Tom felt he was seeing, was a form of what he would call a digital phantasmagoria. It was a digital reflection of him projected on the smartphone screen. It claimed to bear a resemblance to his body, but he could never be sure how accurate the image it produced really was. It raised questions as to what he was really seeing and led him to ask if he could trust his eyes and the phenomenological impressions of his own body, or if the digital representations were more accurate. This question of the relationship between how people know through data and the way this is related to how we can know through our own sensory embodied experience surfaces frequently as we interrogate questions about how we know and learn through self-tracking. Tom's time with his Jawbone ended abruptly on a late June afternoon when he forgot to take the band off his wrist before entering a warm bath after completing a 10 kilometre run. The Jawbone died as it was submerged in water and Tom felt that the mirror in the bathroom along with his own embodied perceptions of his body better reflected his state of well-being than the data emanating from the digital technology. The thought of buying a new Jawbone never crossed his mind, but his time with the Jawbone did propel his curiosity and interest in studying analogue and phenomenological modes of self-tracking and body monitoring.

For a short period of time the wristband became a personal companion that tried to tell us what was going on in and around our moving bodies. Even though it rarely made us exercise more, this device re-conceptualized and transformed our own experiences, physical activities and sleep habits into a language that united us and allowed us to compare and talk about our differences and similarities in navigating the everyday. As it turned out, it was only Vaike who lasted longer than a few months with any device or app, however, all of us stopped using the Jawbone after some months or so like the many other self-trackers who give up with in the first six months. The Jawbone itself did not last either, it was reported as going out of the market in 2017. Indeed, this very reality has also informed our interest in the question of how and why does self-tracking become meaningful enough for people to continue. This has become the key question that has underpinned our conclusions in our research on self-tracking. Nevertheless, tracking ourselves was a significant starting point for the project, we developed our own, although different, sensibilities to the experience of self-tracking and to different devices over the period of the project. From our perspective as ethnographers this gave us the possibility to use our own experiences as a mode of thinking about and seeking to understand the sensory, embodied and emotional feelings of those who participated in our project, and also to discuss these experiences with the participants. It also enabled us to know what sharing our personal data with a group of friends entailed, to know what it felt like reading each other's data and comparing it with our own, even though each of us in the group had such different approaches to exercise that comparison could not be competitive, as it was for some of our participants.

By interrogating our experiences of self-tracking and personal data reflexively in this way we suggest that interdisciplinarity can emerge from research that on the one hand is deeply personal and sensorial and on the other is committed to the writing, theorizing and explication of that experience. All of the authors of this book are experienced ethnographers, but to this question we bring different perspectives that are rooted in our disciplinary expertise. Through design anthropology we have encountered the environmental, sensory, improvisatory and contingent nature of our encounters with technology, contrasted these encounters with the narratives of innovation and markets, and explored imagined futures as well as the experienced present. Through the science of pedagogy we have been able to engage a learning perspective that has shown us how the societal situatedness of technologies and data, and the question of what people really do with technologies, can be fruitfully understood in terms of how we learn to make them part of our lives and how we subsequently imagine them as part of our futures. Through the prism of sociology we have been able to understand how the ideas and assumptions that underpin the design of self-tracking technologies are closely related to social-historical processes of change, such as, for instance, the rise of late modernity, individualization and social acceleration. And, finally, through an ethnological approach we have been able to illuminate how self-tracking technologies become embedded in people's daily lives and routines, and are often linked to and affected by the way older pre-existing technologies inform our understandings and beliefs of what a technology can be used for in new contexts.

We invite readers to join us on an interdisciplinary journey, which offers a way of understanding the multiple and sometimes contesting ways that self-tracking and personal data are imagined to participate, intervene and create change in everyday life, society and our bodies.

1

Self-Tracking in the World

This book explores how self-tracking technologies and personal data have emerged historically, how they participate in our present and how they are shaping and participating in how we envision ourselves and our futures. This temporal approach to self-tracking investigates how both the people who use self-tracking technologies and the designers of these technologies have engaged with them, how they imagine possible individual and societal futures with personal data and the disjunctures and similarities between these imaginaries.

As an increasingly ubiquitous and global everyday form of human engagement with technology and data, self-tracking and personal data present us with an unprecedented view of some of the most vital questions, challenges, opportunities and anxieties that we are faced with as individuals and as a society, as we move into as yet unknown and uncertain human-technological futures. Their presence raises fundamental questions about how it feels – sensorially and emotionally – to live in a world of personal data, how we learn and improvise to engage with the affordances of such a world, and how we give data and technologies meaning.

Imagining Personal Data is for researchers, scholars, students and anyone interested in how self-tracking and personal data are becoming part of how we understand our past, present and future. It is for those who wish to go deeper than what is apparent from the news, marketing and social media hype and use of personal data and self-tracking to ask how they are offering us new ways to think about ourselves and the environments in which we live, and how they enable us to imagine particular possible personal and societal futures. We invite readers to consider with us how we can collectively imagine a route through which these activities, technologies and data can participate in a responsible and ethical future.

We began to investigate self-tracking because we realized that it was fast emerging as a practice with historical, cultural, technological and experiential foundations that was also starting to impact on how we could imagine our personal and technological futures. In 2014, when we first started to ask questions about the meaning of self-tracking, it was only just beginning to become a widespread everyday activity and there existed a limited amount of academic publications on the topic, mainly within informatics and human-computer interaction research traditions through 'e-health and m-health predominantly in health promotion and health communication circles' (Till 2014: 448), which is aligned to behaviour change approaches and other more everyday life-oriented development and design of the technology (Rooksby et al. 2014). During this time there was also an emerging body of literature on self-experimentation with emerging technologies in so-called do-it-yourself biology communities (Seyfried, Pei and Schmidt 2014) and by biohackers (Delfanti 2013). Since then we have seen the use of self-tracking wearables and smartphone apps proceed far beyond the rise of self-tracking communities such as the global Quantified Self (QS) Movement – made up of a loosely tied community of self-trackers whose shared aim is to learn more about themselves through self-tracking – where the early studies of self-tracking itself often began (Neff and Nafus 2016; Lupton 2016a). We have also seen self-tracking become ubiquitous in everyday life contexts beyond the earlier explorations of their applications in everyday health monitoring improvement (Swan 2012). They have since been tested and used – to varying degrees of success – for example, in patient self-care (Lupton 2018), in educational programmes (Williamson 2016; Rich 2017), in direct-to-consumer genetic testing (Ruckenstein 2017), in gaming (Smeddinck et al. 2019), in work life (Moore 2018) and in healthcare insurance (Tu 2019). At the time of writing this book almost five years later, the body of academic literature within this field of study has also grown extensively and approaches self-tracking from multiple perspectives, not the least in relation to questions of data and algorithms and their societal implications, across the social sciences and humanities as well as the fields of technology and design. The growing scholarly interest in practices of, and devices for, self-tracking goes hand in hand with a proliferating interest in these technologies among established and committed self-trackers as well as more casual users that track their everyday activity through smartphone apps, either passively or actively. As we approach the end of the second decade of the twenty-first century, according to their website, the Quantified Self community, often seen as a forerunner in this field, brings together 70,000 people across in the world who are more deeply committed to self-tracking (Quantified Self Institute 2016). According to the Futuresource Wearable Technology Market report (Futuresource Consulting 2018), 24.3 million wearable devices – the wristbands and similar technologies that are worn on the body for self-tracking – were sold during the first quarter of 2018. Although in 2014 it was reported that 'A third of U.S. consumers who have owned one stopped using the device within six months of receiving it' (Endeavour Partners 2014), the implication is that these technologies are an increasingly visible element of everyday life.

As most anthropologists and sociologists are well aware, and as has been evidenced in recent work we have been involved in, neither new technologies nor new forms of data representation change people's behaviour or lead directly to societal change. In the context of research about self-tracking technologies and personal data, social scientists have likewise emphasized how people actively use these devices and representations. For instance, the sociologist Deborah Lupton defines self-tracking broadly as involving 'practices in which people knowingly and purposely collect information about themselves, which they then review and consider applying to the conduct of their lives' (2016a: 2). Lupton's definition, which emphasizes how humans determine the ways they will use data, differs from, for instance, the commercial lingo of marketers and designers of self-tracking devices that often emphasize their potential to support and perhaps also provoke 'behaviour change'. For instance, the designer of the Finnish 'smart' ring ŌURA suggests that 'most of us don't know what's happening in our body' and therefore the ring might 'open a window to the body' through which otherwise invisible aspects of oneself can be seen and known (Berg 2017). In this book, we take Lupton's definition as a starting point, but expand it through our research focus on those less conscious practices of self-tracking whereby people do not necessarily review their personal data and apply their new knowing to how they conduct their lives. As we demonstrate in this book, this expansion reveals the contingent and improvisatory modes through which self-tracking is carried out in everyday life.

In the growing field of disciplinary approaches to self-tracking, critical debates have emerged that are typical of such disciplinary interfaces.

Lupton makes a sociological critique of human–computer interaction (HCI) research, which has tended to be dominated by cognitive or behavioural psychology. In favour of the sociological focus on the social, she argues for highlighting the 'social, cultural and political dimensions' of 'self-tracking cultures' (2014). The sociological critique of how psychological approaches (often adopted in design) focus on the individual and the possibility of 'behaviour change' through awareness or motivation is well established. This offers a convincing response to the HCI self-tracking literature where 'behaviour change' approaches are certainly embedded – for instance, whereby 'self-monitoring has been widely embodied in the design of sensing and monitoring applications because of its effectiveness on increased awareness and behavior change' (Choe et al. 2014: 1144). In ways that align with other sociological responses to behaviour change approaches (e.g. Shove 2010; Strengers 2013), Pantzar and Ruckenstein (2014) have suggested a social practice theory analysis of self-tracking. Indeed, both the critique on neoliberalism that is implicit in a social practice theory approach, which highlights how a behaviour change approach puts responsibility for change on the individual (Shove 2010), and analyses of how self-tracking activity itself becomes implicated in capitalism, suggest that the way we conceptualize the design, use, experience and imaginaries associated with self-tracking technologies and personal data are inevitably political: as Till has suggested, self-tracking can also be understood as a form of 'digital labour', whereby users' exercise and self-tracking can be seen to be supporting commercial organizations, in ways similar to social media, and that it is ultimately 'free labour' which produces data of commercial value (2014: 158). This critique of the neoliberal agenda behind the development of self-tracking has also been highlighted in the history of self-tracking as part of the Do-It-Yourself (DIY) Movement, which is described as a community of people that redefine science into self-experimenting and 'DIY biology' to both democratize science and unleash participatory innovation processes (Meyer 2013). Further, it has been argued that the commercialization of DIY biology, through the connections to test-beds for biotechnological start-ups, has divided the community between rebels who propose open-source and non-profit initiatives and profiteers who want to develop businesses around self-tracking (Seyfried, Pei and Schmidt 2014).

Opening up new directions for self-tracking

As is clear from our discussion, the critique of the place of self-tracking and personal data in contemporary societal structures has been made. Yet less has been said about how we might be able to imagine this change as emerging self-tracking technologies create new possibilities, and as we imagine how self-tracking and personal data might participate in different human futures. This means opening up new possibilities in design. As we have shown in the previous section, changing what people do is not a viable way forward. We emphasize that our approach deliberately avoids falling into the erroneous pattern of seeking to change the behaviour of designers through rational argument. Rather, we propose that the arguments and examples in this book may introduce new ways of thinking in design education, through studio practice. By taking a temporal approach to self-tracking, this book takes a new step to confront precisely how self-tracking and personal data could participate in different human futures. Here, by way of introduction, we invite readers into a moment in our research where such possibilities began to become apparent, specifically through modes of design practice that offer new ways forward.

To explore what departing from such a behaviourist-capitalist agenda could mean in a practical sense, we organized a design workshop on future self-tracking at Halmstad University in Sweden in November 2017. By naming the workshop 'Future Learning with Digital Health Service Design' we wanted to disrupt current design systems of self-tracking and health services by re-thinking such devices as future tools for *learning* instead of as tools for *behavioural change*. What principles and strong concepts underpinning contemporary self-tracking services could and should be questioned to find new ways forward in the development of the next generation of self-tracking devices? And how would the next generation design of self-tracking devices look and function based on alternate principles for why and how they were to be used? To spark the conversation we had invited two experienced and influential self-trackers – Thomas Blomseth Christiansen and Jakob Eg Larsen from the global QS community – to give their take on the current situation as well as next steps forward. In their talk they presented the One Button Tracker (see Figure 1.1), a low-tech device, to open up technological possibilities for paying attention to subjective experiences of daily living.

Figure 1.1 Prototype of the One Button Tracker – design of a future self-tracking device for tracking subjective experiences by Thomas Blomseth Christiansen and Jakob Eg Larsen (published with permission).

The design of the One Button Tracker was based on the following principles: it is at hand when needed, it can be operated without looking at it, it automatically keeps time, it stores data reliably, it exposes data via a wire, it generates easily understood data and it only turns on when in use. In short, it is a device that has a button that you can push, and thereby create a timestamp, whenever you experience something in your body that you want to pay attention to. According to Blomseth Christiansen and Eg Larsen, these principles mirrored what was needed to create the 'infinite instrument' for *active* self-tracking, that is self-tracking that is designed to help people notice things about themselves from a subjective perspective, in opposition to more conventionally designed self-tracking instruments that measure the body from an imagined objective stance. Blomseth Christiansen is widely known for tracking his every sneeze for five years in order to cure himself of allergies and eczema through long-running experiments with his lifestyle. In the process he collected a unique data-set of over 100,000 observations, and in this process he has become a strong advocate for shifting perspectives from self-tracking *of* the body, to a more subjective practice of paying attention to experiences *in* self-tracking and how this experience changes over time when you, through the tracking, learn more about how to pay attention to the experience you want to track.

In many ways this shift in perspectives exemplifies this book's contribution through its conceptualization of self-tracking as an everyday and design practice, whereby there is a shift from understanding it as the passive monitoring of bodily activities (body monitoring) to understanding it as the active tracking of subjective experiences. Self-tracking technologies and the personal data they produce have become ubiquitous in our lives and promise to be inseparable from our futures. The assumptions that underpin approaches that simply see them as offering increased self-knowledge, improving health, and a life that, often in quite a vaguely defined way, is imagined to be 'better', need to be revised. The question is how people learn to live together with these devices, how the devices become part of how people orient themselves in their pursuit to move through their everyday lives, and what the implications of this are for their future imaginaries. As we outline in the next section, this also means a shift to a research approach that accounts for the *experience* of self-tracking and personal data.

The everyday realities of self-tracking and personal data

The idea that self-tracking should be viewed and discussed in broader terms than suggested through a quantifying research agenda is now well established both inside and outside academia. Outside academia, the QS community devoted their international conference 2018 to the intersection between the 'Quantified Self-method' (that is, making observations of yourself, analysing them and making conclusions) and formal and informal learning. By stating that 'all Quantified Self projects aim at learning', this group of early and advanced adopters pushes the scope of self-tracking beyond ideas of self-tracking as solely quantifying body activities to create behavioural change, into a social, cultural and societal direction with the aim to 'contribute to this expanded understanding of what it means to learn, and to help the culture of everyday science grow as a force for change' (Quantified Self Labs n.d.). In the same vein, academic research in the social sciences and humanities has shown that, for people who use trackers, self-tracking is *not* solely about measuring the body in terms of quantities and collecting data for statistical analysis according to a rational and scientific agenda (Lupton 2016a; Neff and Nafus 2016; Ajana 2018; Brogård Kristensen and Ruckenstein 2018).

As a example, consider the experiences of Chris Dancy – the 'most connected man in the world' (Dancy n.d.) – who has used sensor technologies to track and measure almost every aspect of his everyday life. In a short video linked to his website Chris shows the filmmakers around his home, explaining to them how he has used technologies that he makes invisible or hidden from others, to monitor as much detail of his life as possible. This has included ingestible, wearable and location-based sensors, voice-recording devices, apps and services, connected devices such as digital scales and every light bulb connected to the internet individually, a sleep monitor and more. He tells the filmmaker that when he checked in about 2014, there had been something like 20,000 things measuring his life. We meet Chris again later in this book: his example is one where self-tracking and digital health come together in perhaps extreme but also novel and effective ways, and indeed creates a public and practical narrative for self-tracking that coincides with many aspects of our argument. To explain what it was like living in a world of data where nearly 'everything' was tracked, Chris told Sarah about a period when he had taken time out from this tracking:

> Chris: I didn't take off sensors until I went to a retreat in 2015 and then I took off everything and that was kind of mind blowing – not taking them off, but putting them back on.
>
> Sarah: So you stopped completely then?
>
> Chris: For a week I went to a 10 day silent Buddhist retreat … I'd been meditating and someone had suggested to me that a silent retreat would be enlightening, and the most I'd meditated before up to that

point was three or four hours, straight, like in one sitting, I'd never done eight hours a day, so I really wanted to understand what it was that's so amazing about this, you know and as I said taking the sensors off wasn't hard, putting them back on was … it was terrible the first couple of days. I felt like I feel the data you know, it's one thing to track and to have a lot of automation in your tracking, its another thing to take it off … everyone said … won't you be nervous or … you'd be so relieved when you take it off, it was actually effortless to take everything off and there were no clocks at the retreat, there were no books, there was nothing to read, it was easy, I mean if you go into a pretty timeless environment, coming out of that timeless environment is hard … the first thing I noticed when I was putting on … was how sad everyone was … after I left the retreat and my friend took me into an San Francisco I just started looking around at how … distracted everyone was, and that made me feel really sad and I hadn't checked my email or put my phone back on yet, but I'd put my watch back on … [it made him think:] Oh, it's heavy to be alive.

Sarah: And you said you could feel the data.

Chris: I felt as I put on each thing and turned on each system (how many systems were there then … how many things).

While Chris's life was highly quantified, as his discussion explains, this simultaneously created an experiential environment, where data is 'felt' emotionally and sensorially. It is this aspect of self-tracking, which comes to the fore so clearly in this description, that is often overlooked.

Existing research has begun to account for the everyday realities of what people do and feel with personal data to a certain extent. For instance, as we mentioned in the introduction to this chapter, it has been argued that markets for self-tracking technologies are constituted through the emergence and maintenance of social 'practices' (Pantzar and Ruckenstein 2014). A focus on the social is useful in its emphasis on the processual nature of life and on the non-representational ways of knowing that constitute the practice or 'doing' of everyday activity. However, we wish to push this further, to beyond looking at how practices emerge and can be seen to pattern social activity, and life. Further to this we are concerned with the contingencies of everyday life, the individual modes of improvisation that give meaning to our uses of technology and the feelings that are part of these configurations. Attending to the social is important, since as we show social relations of self-tracking are inseparable from the feelings involved in self-tracking and, indeed, participate in their constitution. However, we also need to engage analytically with the detail and variation of what individuals do in order to see how body monitoring becomes entangled in everyday lives and worlds. As the ethnographic work of anthropologists Nafus and Sherman shows, the individual and diverse ways that body-monitoring technologies are used is essential to understanding their implications. Nafus and Sherman point out that 'attempts to elicit participation in coordinated studies within QS have rarely succeeded because people have such wildly different ideas about what constitutes an interesting measurement' (2014: 1791). Indeed, anthropological attention to the individual recognizes the place of individuals in research as unique moving and perceiving beings, always co-implicated in the worlds they are part of. This brings to the fore the situated and contingent nature of digital media use (Pink and Leder Mackley 2013), which implies the importance of accounting for body monitoring as unfolding in different ways as digital media, technologies, representations and biographical and in-the-moment human embodied experience become variously entangled in everyday environments. It has also been argued that the field of personal informatics within HCI research needs to account for 'the way personal tracking is enmeshed with everyday life and people's outlook on their future' (Rooksby et al. 2014: 1163). Rooksby and colleagues introduce the concept of *lived informatics* to open up a discussion that moves beyond the idea of people simply as users who collect data for a specific purpose to the notion of people as wayfarers in information for the purpose of a life being lived. They take up the concepts of dwelling and wayfaring developed by anthropologist Tim Ingold (2000), which emphasize the processual and emergent nature of people's interactions with their environments. Ingold contends that skills of perception are developed through people's experiences in the context of their surroundings. Rooksby and colleagues adopt this perspective when they argue that 'when people track their activities (when they dwell in data) they are not building a description of their lives, but are wayfaring in information – knowing oneself may involve collecting and reflecting on information about oneself but is for the purposes of a life being lived' (2014: 1171). To understand how this plays out as a process through which humans continually and incrementally engage with and know in the world, we will outline a learning approach to self-tracking and personal data. First, however, we set the scene further through an overview of how personal data can be understood from a humanities and social science perspective.

Understanding personal data

Scholars in the humanities and social sciences have explored, sought to define and, indeed, also played with creative interpretations of what data might mean in historic as well as present and future contexts (for instance, Kitchin 2014; Gitelman 2013). In contrast to understanding data as pre-factual and pre-analytical, data are increasingly regarded as 'inherently partial, selective and representative' and dependent on their selection criteria (Kitchin 2014). As Bowker (2005:184) has put it, '"raw data" is both an oxymoron and a bad idea'. Instead, as Kitchin (2014) rightly points out, data are always both social and material by having certain forms and being situated in different contexts, and these factors are important for how data are shaped, how they can be processed, transformed, stored and distributed. Importantly, data do not represent the world but become part of the processes and practices that shape it. A growing number of researchers from the humanities and social sciences have questioned what Van Dijck (2014) labels dataism, 'a widespread belief in the objective quantification and potential tracking of all kinds of human behavior and sociality'. In doing so they have pointed to the need for studying the practices by which data are identified, gathered, exchanged and automated (Van Dijck 2014; Schäfer and Van Es 2017). Further, as Iliadis and Russo point out, the concept of data itself is 'always-already constituted within wider data assemblages' and operating under existing epistemological and power structures, 'inflect[ing] and interact[ing] with society, its organization and functioning, and the resulting impact on individuals' daily lives' (2016: 1).

Data treated as objective representations of an activity or dimension of people's bodies and selves can lead to poorly informed data-driven policy or data-driven design, in that it is based on an understanding of past, present or future realities that do not account for the contexts, trajectories and inaccuracies of the data. Such assumptions lead to rather naive and instrumentalist uses of data to describe what is happening or to seek to predict what might happen in the future in ways that are inevitably incomplete and inaccurate. Indeed, scholars in the field of critical data studies (Iliadis and Russo 2016) have begun to interrogate the meaning of data and to offer alternative understandings of data as always incomplete and unfinished. Here, scholars have problematized assumptions about what data can mean and the kinds of value that can be apportioned to it (Boyd and Crawford 2012; Markham 2013; Manovich 2013; Kitchin 2014; Nafus 2014).

This has led to the use of a number of metaphors which in common seek to define data as part of the continuity of the world we live in and as emergent with the organic and processual lives of humans and our environment, rather than as an objective representation of life in a world that data can be separated from. Therefore, for example, from an anthropological perspective, Boellstorff (2013) has theorized big data as 'rotted data' in order to reflect 'how data can be transformed in parahuman, complexly material, and temporally emergent ways that do not always follow a preordained, algorithmic "recipe"'. The sociologist Lupton has coined the idea that data are 'lively' to discuss the many ways in which data are 'vital', in that 'they are fundamentally about the lives of humans: about their bodily functions, behaviours, social relationships, moods and emotions' (2016a: 5) and to signal when data are no longer used how they might be 'dying, dead, decaying, ageing, dirty, contaminated, worn out or sick' (Pink et al. 2018). In existing work about self-tracking we have also found it useful to engage with the science and technology studies (STS) concept of breakage and broken world theory (Jackson 2014) to describe data as 'broken' (Pink et al. 2018).

Approaching self-tracking as a practice and as happening within an experiential world requires an exploration of how data and processes of datafication are imagined. As a practice, self-tracking has evolved as part of a 'metric culture', which Ajana proposes 'indicates at once a growing cultural interest in numbers, as well as a culture that is increasingly shaped and populated with numbers' (2018: 2–3), and as part of an evolution of what anthropologists have called 'audit cultures' (Strathern 2000; Wright and Shore 2015), which bring to the fore the institutionalization, politics and power relations of the use of personal data. In many cases, self-tracking is closely related to processes of datafication through which bodily activities, characteristics and measurements are reconstituted into networked quantified data as 'actionable sites of value and insight' that are believed to allow for real-time tracking and predictive analysis (Cukier and Mayer-Schoenberger 2013). Understood as a 'conversion of qualitative aspects of life into quantified data' (Ruckenstein and Schüll 2017: 261) or as 'the ability to render into data many aspects of the world that have not been quantified before' (Cukier and Mayer-Schoenberger 2013), processes of datafication often rely on the possibility to quantify what is otherwise complex and hard to transform into numbers. Instead of focusing on the systems as such, an increasing number of researchers within the social sciences and humanities have emphasized the importance of studying the practices by which such data are identified, gathered, exchanged and automated (Van Dijck 2014; Schäfer and Van Es 2017).

As the above indicates, personal data covers a wide range of possible sets of data about people, their bodies and lives. Our interest lies in a specific type of personal data – that which is generated through the use of self-tracking technologies. However, this kind of personal data does not exist in isolation from other personal data, and indeed it is likely that in the future it will become increasingly integrated and possible to easily aggregate (from the individual user's perspective) with an increasing range of other data sources. As we see from the examples of some of the most committed self-trackers, aggregating self-tracking data with other data sources is already possible but requires a high degree of personal commitment to the collection and analysis of those data. As the title of this book indicates, we advocate an understanding of personal data as something that not only *can* be imagined but indeed *must* be imagined in order to count as data. Rather than approaching data as pre-factual and always already existent, we argue that data become meaningful in relation to the practices through which our everyday lives are played out.

Learning with self-tracking technologies and personal data

Our approach to self-tracking and personal data is *processual*, that is, we are interested in how self-tracking plays out as a process through which humans continually and incrementally engage with and know in the world to make it become meaningful in relation to the historical, social, material and mundane context we call everyday life. In this process, learning is inevitable, and we are interested in the pedagogies – the *learning cultures and strategies* – people develop when self-tracking devices comes into their lives. In health and personal informatics research there is growing interest in pedagogical perspectives on digital self-tracking, which has been channelled through didactic discussions around what and how these devices 'teach' the user. Within these interconnected fields, Lomborg and Frandsen (2016) have identified two major strands of self-tracking research that are based in the intersection between computer science (and in particular HCI) and health studies. These strands respond to the following type of questions: (a) how can self-tracking encourage and empower users to change their behaviours to develop a healthier lifestyle (see, for example, Swan 2012; Wang et al. 2014) and (b) how can the design of self-tracking technologies be optimized to motivate a specific user experience and an associated behaviour deemed beneficial to the user (see Kim 2014)? In the case of self-tracking devices related to improving human health, fitness and well-being, personal data already have a defined meaning and value attached to them as part of the rationales for use that have been decided by corporate or state actors. There is an overt pedagogical imperative included in the design, promotion and marketing of self-tracking devices, often to the point that it is deemed appropriate that people are 'pushed' or 'nudged' into using them for their own good (Lupton 2015; Lupton 2016a; Schüll 2016). When these devices are directed at self-monitoring aspects of people's bodies in the interests of encouraging them to learn about their biometrics and act on their data to improve their health, they act in bio-pedagogical ways, building on the tradition in previous eras of health education efforts to encourage people to change their behaviours for the sake of their health (Rich and Miah 2014; Lupton 2015; Fotopoulou and O'Riordan 2017). However, it would be all too easy to reduce self-tracking to a question of Foucauldian biopolitics or a question of how these devices act as pedagogies (Giroux 2004) in the sense that the health technology market 'teaches' us how to increase our well-being through mainly negative ideological forces that act upon and even corrupt individuals (see Purpura et al. 2011). We argue that viewing self-tracking from perspectives that are all too technologically deterministic in nature runs the risk of failing to appreciate the fact that there is more at stake here than issues of discipline, power and people being blindly steered by the potentials and allure of new technologies.

The idea that we encounter the world through incremental and often non-cognitive processes of learning and knowing is well established in anthropology and in branches of pedagogy, including our own work (Pink 2015; Fors, Bäckström and Pinks 2013). Pink's concept of digital wayfaring (Hjorth and Pink 2014) enables us to consider not only how people dwell in the personal data that is produced through self-tracking (Rooksby et al. 2014), but how they learn as they move through a digital material environment. To explain how people learn and know about themselves with self-tracking technologies this book engages four themes that build on this approach. The first theme places a particular focus on the *sensoriality of self-tracking* and the modes of unspoken, sensory and embodied as well as visualized and verbalized learning that make it meaningful. The second theme highlights the *spatiality of self-tracking*, and how the activities and technologies are inseparable from the material, technological, sensory and intangible environments with which they emerge. The third theme examines the *technological possibilities of self-tracking* in relation to the social, cultural and historical contexts in which self-tracking technologies are developed, designed and used. Finally, the fourth theme focuses on *improvisations in self-tracking*, that is, how people find new ways of using their self-tracking devices, data and develop practices in relation to the contingencies that shape everyday situations. In Chapter 2 we elaborate on our learning approach and these four themes.

Unfolding self-tracking and personal data

In the following chapters our discussion of self-tracking and personal data unfolds through a discussion that begins in Chapter 2 with an outline of the theoretical and methodological commitments that shape our discussions, and the temporal and learning approaches we take. In Chapter 3 we examine aspects of the past of self-tracking, through a focus on the mirror and to a lesser extent the weighing scale, both of which were to later become, and are currently, ubiquitous technologies. Existing research into the past temporalities of self-tracking has included explorations of the histories or 'precursors' of self-tracking, suggesting that it is a historically rooted activity. Nafus and Neff, who suggest that 'we have always been quantified', highlight that in the United States Benjamin Franklin (the statesman) tracked his life through his diaries in the eighteenth century and Buckminster Fuller (a mid-twentieth-century inventor) recorded his activities every fifteen minutes (Nafus and Neff 2016: 15); Humphreys suggests that the diary keeping and sharing of earlier centuries offers us a mode of understanding both accounts and forms of accountability regarding ordinary everyday life, which throws light on contemporary uses of social media whereby people share what they have eaten, seen on TV or the birth of a baby on Facebook or Twitter, and post photos on Instagram (2018: 2–3) and that stands for a kind of 'qualified self', which can be considered a form of self-tracking (22). Our focus on the mirror foregrounds our subsequent discussions of how the representational and informational aspects of self-tracking technologies on the one hand, and its sensory and felt experiences on the other, were articulated as part of everyday personal, social and spatial environments.

During the four years of our research we witnessed the ongoing processes of technology design and marketing, as they emerged alongside the everyday realities of veteran and committed self-trackers as well as of people we call everyday self-trackers, who do so mainly for their personal interest, perhaps alone or with one or two others, and do not necessarily follow the conventions of organizations such as QS. As we outline in Chapter 4, which focuses on self-tracking through an interrogation of the technology, an existing literature around this has grown up in HCI sociology as well as science and technology studies. Whereas the first field of studies has a long history of approaching life-logging through the perspective of persuasive computing, i.e. technologies that are designed to change people's 'behaviours', the latter fields of studies have to a larger extent approached self-tracking from a critical perspective that understands self-tracking technologies partly as invested with certain ideologies, values and assumptions, and partly as becoming material participants in the everyday life of people where they intervene, affect and push people in certain programmed directions.

In this book we take the new step of considering such questions alongside our ethnographic studies of self-trackers in Chapter 5. Thus considering the narratives of what technology design expects and 'wants' people to do and feel with self-tracking technologies, in juxtaposition with the question of what different groups of users actually do, know and experience with such technologies.

By taking a spatial and learning approach to self-tracking, we emphasize both the movement that self-tracking entails and the continually emergent nature of the way we learn and know through self-tracking technologies. We emphasize the ongoing slipping over of the present into the immediate and then more distant past, and account for the ability to imagine the possible but always uncertain futures of self-tracking. Such futures are imagined differently by different stakeholders in the self-tracking scene. Everyday self-trackers, QS members, technology designers and companies as well as insurance and other organizations have different views on the future of self-tracking, which variously encompass human experience, the technological possibilities of emerging technologies and the markets they might generate or appeal to. For policy-makers there are moreover other future imaginaries, where self-tracking technologies might be associated with future forms as diverse as those of societal governance and regulation or of public health. In Chapter 6 we explore this context to understand how self-tracking futures are envisaged from the different perspectives of QS veterans and everyday users, and the possibilities of emerging technologies. Finally, in Chapter 7 we draw together the findings of the previous chapters to propose an agenda for the future of research and design for self-tracking technologies and personal data.

2

Encountering the Temporalities and Imaginaries of Personal Data

In this chapter we present our approach to self-tracking as part of a processual world, which manifests, intersects and sometimes is contested in different past, present and future temporalities and imaginaries. Existing research discussed in Chapter 1 has equipped us with ways of understanding the embodied, sociotechnical and societal questions and relations of self-tracking and personal data. We now build on this by engaging concepts of emergence, learning, knowing and imagination to outline an interdisciplinary design anthropological approach to self-tracking and personal data. We then introduce the four themes – sensoriality, spatiality, technological possibility and human improvisation – which we use as prisms into how self-tracking and personal data are experienced and contribute to learning in everyday life. Following this we explain how we encountered these themes through historical, reflexive, collaborative, object-oriented and future-focused methodologies.

Design anthropology is, as Smith and Otto have put it, 'a *distinct way of knowing*, one which incorporates both analysis and intervention in the process of constructing knowledge' (2016: 19; italics in original). Design anthropology does not represent one single theory or mode of doing research. Rather, it brings the two disciplines of anthropology and design together in various ways, including the anthropology of design, anthropology to inform design and anthropological engagements with design that both challenge and shift the practice of both disciplines. Design anthropology can be thought of as developing in three 'waves', which have developed approaches that focus respectively on social and interactional aspects of technology design and use (Suchman 1998; Vinkhuyzen and Cefkin 2016: 522–523); material culture studies perspectives and object design (Clarke 2017); and a phenomenological approach that is rooted in processual theories of creativity, emergence, possibility and intervention (Ingold 2012; 2013; Halse 2013; Gunn and Donovan 2012; Gunn, Otto and Smith 2013; Smith et al. 2016; Pink et al. 2016; Akama et al. 2018). Our argument in this book participates in the development of this third wave, drawing on our earlier discussions of a design anthropology of emerging technologies – self-tracking devices and autonomous driving vehicles (Pink et al. 2017; 2018; Pink and Fors 2017) – and situating a learning approach to self-tracking (Fors and Pink 2017) further within a temporal approach. In particular our design anthropological approach exceeds the brief of conventional single discipline social science and humanities research as follows:

First, in the subject matter of our research and in our intentions: we study how design happens in technology design contexts, how design does not end when users take over technologies but continues through their use, and we consider our work in itself to be an intervention. However, the nature of our intervention in this book is not what would be assumed for conventional applied research, to inform or collaborate in a particular process of product or service design in the self-tracking technology industry or market. Rather, we seek to intervene by advancing a new theory of self-tracking, what it can mean, how it can have enduring and future benefits for users, that is also responsible and ethical.

Second, in our commitment to interdisciplinarity in theory and method: while our work is closer to anthropology than to design, our social science approach is inflected by the temporalities of design in our focus on the imagination and on the possible futures of self-tracking both in relation to research participants' own imagined personal futures and the imaginations of designers. However, our project is further interdisciplinary in drawing from our (the authors') disciplinary training in pedagogy, anthropology, sociology and ethnology. In order to tackle the question at the core of our work – why do people make a commitment to self-tracking, and how can this become part of a responsible and ethical mode of future living with digital data? – we do not keep to a single discipline perspective but weave our argument through four themes – sensoriality, spatiality, technological possibility and human improvisation – that enable us to bring together insights from each of these disciplinary fields.

In what follows we first outline our theoretical and interventional research agenda and then discuss how these four themes serve as a bridge through which it can be mobilized as a methodology and set of techniques for doing research about the past, present and futures of self-tracking and personal data.

An interdisciplinary design anthropological approach to self-tracking

Our theoretical understanding of self-tracking is constructed around three interconnected concepts – emergence, imagination and learning. It is based on the principles that humans live and learn with technologies within continually emergent environments of which those technologies are also part (Fors and Pink 2017), and that people's experiences of technologies in the everyday circumstances of the continually shifting present are what enable us to imagine, fear or have hopes in as yet unknowable futures (Pink, Fors and Glöss 2017). We argue that human–technology relations need to be understood beyond the study of the sociotechnical, to instead situate people and technology as part of shared environments, that they participate in the constitution of. This means researching beyond the person–technology relationship or interaction (which is the focus of some sociological and much HCI research) to also attend to the materiality, sensoriality, sociality and the intangible elements of how people are part of everyday environments and the everyday sensations and emotions that are afforded as they become entangled in our lives and activities.

A theory of *emergence* is central to contemporary design anthropology (for example, Smith and Otto 2016; Akama et al. 2018), which is committed to processual theories of the world, rooted in phenomenological anthropology, that acknowledge the emergent and often visibly changing nature of the everyday worlds we live and research in. Smith and Otto posit that 'The question of emergent cultural and social realities poses a major challenge to anthropology today' (2016: 21). The challenge requires us to ethnographically encounter subject matter that is always in the process of coming about and not ever finished. Of course, this is not an empirical change in the world itself but, rather, a theoretical position which means that we must research and learn with processes that are ongoing, and acknowledge that when our research ends these processes continue; and that we have an opportunity to use what we have learnt to comment on and seek to intervene in what might happen next. A theory of emergence moreover suggests that our research has not only taken place in a temporality that is relegated to the ethnographic past (cf. Löfgren and Willim 2005; O'Dell 2013), but has reached out to how participants and ourselves have anticipated self-tracking futures. Likewise, the writing of this book is an anticipatory action through which we seek to continue our dialogues about self-tracking, and not a text in which we wish to close these down into the past.

Therefore, a theory of emergence enables us to take up the question of futures in ways that neither anthropology nor the other social science and humanities disciplines that our work connects with have conventionally managed. Our engagement with design anthropology is a first step in this attention to futures, since, unlike traditional research approaches in the social sciences that have rendered everything that is knowable to research to the past, design has had to confront futures, since design as a discipline is involved in what will happen next as much as what is happening now. Social science's struggle with the question of the present and future has been discussed in detail elsewhere in our own work (for example, Pink, Fors and O'Dell 2017; Pink and Salazar 2017), as have the ethical implications of shifting the temporalities of ethnographic engagements (Pink 2017). Here we note, however, that the move from the study of the past to that of the future marks an important step for the social sciences, and one that enables us to more adeptly and confidently participate in discussions about design and to become more interventional in our stance (O'Dell 2013). In inviting us to the future, a theory of emergence as outlined above also reminds us of the contingency of the past, present and future (see Irving 2017) that our research process and practice has moved between. It points out to us that futures are uncertain and that to recognize them as such has implications for both researchers and designers (Pink and Akama 2015).

The concept of *imagination* became central to our research, since to understand what self-tracking and personal data are *for* we needed to understand how they were part of the way that people imagined themselves. This involved considering how people's uses and experiences are embedded in historical processes and the specificities of contemporary everyday environments through which socially and culturally specific modes of technology use have developed, and in how these are moreover inseparable from the ways in which technologies are imagined by their designers. Thus, our research has engaged with a triple intersection of imagination: the imagination of the users of self-tracking technologies as they improvise with them to accomplish their everyday life objectives and needs; the imaginations of technology designers and marketers concerning how and why people will use their technologies and the assumptions that these are based on; and the imagination of the researcher, both to empathetically engage with the imaginary worlds of others and in something akin to the sociological imagination, as we turn this work into an analytical discussion. In this sense we understand and use the imagination to refer to how the users of self-tracking technologies consider their futures as non-determinate (see Sneath, Holbraad and Pedersen 2009), in that imagination does not project things that will happen, but enables us to think in terms of possibilities. As an everyday anticipatory mode imagination is also part of how we trust, hope and believe in personal data: it is how we make it meaningful to ourselves as we consider our past–present–future temporalities as we move through time. Therefore, in writing about the imagination, we do not assume that there is a future out there waiting to be imagined but, rather, like technologies and their relationships with humans, we see imagination as emergent from specific circumstances. It is therefore important for us to understand these circumstances and to be able to assess what their consequences might be.

When speaking of the ways that the future of self-tracking technologies are imagined in technology fields, marketing and other popular public narratives, we are working with a different mode of imagining futures. The future imaginaries of these narratives are predictive and quantitative and envision futures in which technologies are expected to impact on individuals and societies, as discussed in Chapter 4. They run contrary to the theory of emergence that guides our research. Yet they exist in society and are indeed the drivers of innovation initiatives, of funding for projects that hope that giving people health-monitoring technologies will result in them changing their behaviour and improving their health. These narratives and the modes of representation through which they exist in society are part of the worlds we live in, in which people use self-tracking technologies and where academics work. If we now consider how imagination becomes implicated in these processes of making everyday life and design happen, then we can consider imagination as an anticipatory mode that is emergent from the circumstances of the everyday that we have described. Yet the imaginaries of the future of self-tracking that circulate in media and other representations also participate in constituting these circumstances. Part of living with personal data involves learning how to navigate this world where different modes of imagining futures coincide.

Finally, a theory of *learning* and *knowing* underpins our research; similarly to our understanding of the imagination, this is informed by our understanding of the world and what happens in it as continually emergent. Our approach to learning and knowing implies a shift in perspective, which re-thinks the pedagogical elements of self-tracking, away from the question of what we might *know about* our activities through self-tracking technologies, towards that of what we might *learn with* them. This means taking a different pedagogical lens, which explores how self-tracking technologies can become resources for learning within our lives (not about them) and highlights what it is that we actually learn when using them. Our ethnographic approach invites us to account for the experience of living in a world of personal data, identifying the ways in which these data become constituted and incorporated into everyday life as part of routine practices. Importantly, personal data may be alternatively ignored, disregarded or resisted, deemed as lacking interest or value or as inciting negative emotions. Our approach also offers us ways to explore the experiential qualities of data as they are materialized. That is, understanding the visualization of data as information from its privileged position as 'knowledge', towards emphasizing the greater relevance of how people come to know through their experiences of data when they are materialized in various ways. By making this shift, we not only question the idea that personal data information is equivalent to knowledge per se, but also the way generating personal data may be perceived as a hunt for objective knowledge that by revealing it to users through effective digital interfaces automatically will provide them with a tool for learning through behavioural change. As we have outlined in Chapter 1 and above, we suggest that personal data that is generated through self-tracking is more than an opportunity for behavioural change. On a social and cultural level, self-tracking entails learning to live with data and, as Chun (2016) points out, media (including personal data) matters the most when they seem not to matter at all in terms of novelty and capacities – when they have moved from 'new' to habitual.

In moving beyond understandings of self-tracking from primarily promoting human behaviour change by providing the right feedback and motivation factors though a digital interface, we advocate for the use of a processual learning theory that articulates how knowledge is an embodied way of being-in-the-world (Merleau-Ponty 1962), emplaced (Howes 2005), situated in everyday activities (Lave and Wenger 1991) and part of how these activities are perceived (Ingold 2000). By doing this, we contribute to a growing body of research that both situates the use of digital technology devices in relation to the body and investigates how this use becomes part of people's ongoing and ever-changing embodied relationship with their digital material and experiential surroundings (see, for example, Fors 2015; Fors and Pink 2017). This perspective informs our ethnographic approach to understanding people as sensory and emplaced learners (see Fors, Bäckström and Pink 2013) whose ways of learning, knowing and moving through the world are entangled with their uses of digital body-monitoring devices and the environments of which people and technologies are both part. Here, learning and knowing become incremental, contingent and situated rather than predetermined or possible to detach from the knower. These perspectives help us to understand how people come to participate in the formation of knowing and meaning through data through the recognition that learning is *lived* and enacted by people in diverse and changing social, historic and material contexts.

From theory to method: Four themes

To investigate learning as lived in this way we have emphasized four themes, which underpin our understanding of how self-tracking and personal data are experienced. These themes bind together the conceptual, empirical and methodological levels of our work and are the sites for dialogue between them. In this section we outline how they are evidenced conceptually and empirically. The next section demonstrates how they are embedded in our methods.

The embodied sensoriality of self-tracking

Self-tracking can accompany us through every moment and situation in our day, it gets close to our embodiment and to our ways of sensing and being-in-the-world, and it becomes implicated in our personal relationships. Through self-tracking the significance of hardware, data and algorithms can be felt sensorially and emotionally. In Chapter 1 we emphasized how self-tracking and personal data is 'felt' by introducing Chris Dancy's experience of taking a break from self-tracking. Everyday self-trackers also acknowledged such experiences. For example, one of our Australian participants, a man in his thirties working in the IT industry, explained the experience of wearing his Fitbit to Sarah, describing how he liked his own Fitbit because he used it with a clip, which meant he could keep it in his pocket or clip it onto his belt, with the option of using a wristband when he was asleep. The way he wore the Fitbit impacted both on how it felt on his body and how he felt about the data it produced. As he explained:

> Basically I just don't like having stuff on my hands and I know there's a couple of people at work who do have the wristband on and I know that when they move their arms that counts as a step, whereas mine, my entire body has to move … and I want it to be accurate, there's no point in just measuring how much I wave my arm.

Like other participants he interpreted the data produced with his wearable, specifically in relation to the way he personally wore and used the wearable. His understanding of the data was not simply quantitative but was always imbued with what he sensed about how it was made.

We place a particular focus on such sensorial elements of self-tracking and the modes of unspoken, sensory and embodied as well as visualized and verbalized knowing and learning made self-tracking meaningful. Our research included people who use self-tracking devices in ways that are not intended, who start and stop for different reasons and who actively resist certain types of self-tracking. An emphasis on the sensory brings to the fore the continually emergent relationship of our experience and engagement with technologies and data, the idea that the modes through which we imagine futures can be embodied, unspoken and 'felt' or sensed, and that knowing and learning with self-tracking technologies and personal data are likewise concerned with such feelings.

The spatiality of self-tracking

Self-tracking and personal data are always experienced in places and are often co-constitutive of our experience of place. That is, the activities and technologies of self-tracking are inseparable from the material, technological, sensory and intangible environments with which they emerge and they contribute to our experiences of these places. In Chapter 1, Chris Dancy's experience showed us the importance of attending to how the materiality and technology of the everyday environment make new ways of knowing about ourselves and our bodies both possible and representational. This also applies to historical examples of measuring and monitoring the body, and to the ways that people imagine self-tracking as part of their environments in the future.

Contemporary self-tracking happens across diverse everyday environments and, as argued elsewhere (Pink and Fors 2017), personal data can be seen as emerging through the relationship between humans, technologies and aspects of the outdoor environment, including the ground underfoot, the weather and the built environment. Thus, as we see public space as increasingly 'datafied' (Sumartojo et al. 2016), we begin to imagine futures where sensor technologies and new modes of automation will diversify both the forms of data that can be produced and shared in and about such environments and to contemplate the ethics and responsibilities that this will raise. Weight or sleep tracking are often or usually undertaken in the home, a site where many of the things that are important to our identities and everyday routines happen (for example, Miller 2001; Pink 2004; Pink et al. 2017). Such self-tracking data is created through our relationships with the material, sensory and social environments of our homes. Understanding self-tracking technologies and data as part of the materialities and technologies of homes suggests that personal data can become enduringly significant to people precisely because it is bound up with the other everyday materialities and routines that people need to be engaged with in order to accomplish their everyday objectives. As for public space, the idea that self-tracking and personal data in homes will increasingly intersect in an progressively datafied future with automated smart-home technologies invites us to attend to how these futures can be imagined and accounted for. In the following chapters we set self-tracking technologies, and the individual and societal meanings that may be associated with them, within the spatial relations and environments through which they produce data.

The technological possibilities of self-tracking

Part of our agenda to provide a new alternative to the dominant narratives that claim that self-tracking technologies can bring about beneficial technologically driven behaviour change involves putting people at the centre of the analysis. To do this we understand self-tracking technologies (and technologies more broadly) through the concept of technological possibilities. In Chapter 3 we ask how ubiquitous technologies for monitoring and measuring the body and self became part of everyday practices historically, to explore how the possibilities technologies afford shift over time. For instance, the history of materials that became first glass and then the mirror were entwined with how people came to see and monitor themselves and others. The technological possibilities of the mirror did not alone lead to changes in perception of the self, but rather they participated in societal processes through which individuals developed modes of use for them. The mirror is particularly pertinent since it has continued to occupy a prominent place in contemporary society, whereby it is resituated in relation to the modes of seeing and knowing of contemporary self-tracking technologies. In Chapter 4 we push this exploration further by putting the design intent of contemporary self-tracking apps at the centre of our analysis in order to examine and problematize a context where these technologies seem to 'want' their users to participate in a particular relationship with them. As we demonstrate, what self-tracking technologies want can likewise be understood in relation to particular societal narratives, discourses and structures.

Improvisation in self-tracking

At the core of design anthropology is the attention on how people improvise in relation to the contingencies that shape everyday situations. This approach builds on the work of Ingold and Hallam (2007) who have emphasized the continuity of human creativity. Following Ingold and Hallam's argument, we can contrast the improvisatory nature of the creative modes of engagement that people develop as they learn to use self-tracking technologies and personal data, with the narratives of innovation that see technologies as closed and finished products which will impact on people and society. This is a key difference between our design anthropological approach whereby we see self-tracking technologies and personal data as opening up possibilities with which people might improvise and the behaviour change approaches we have critiqued in Chapter 1, which suggests that technologies can intervene to change what people do. Our ethnographic work has revealed examples of improvisation across different types of users of self-tracking technologies and personal data.

For example, Chris Dancy was an extraordinary self-tracker both in the detail of his tracking and the ways that he improvised to track himself and to rethink the design of self-tracking itself. In his aim to track 'everything' Chris appropriated existing smartphone sensors and apps as well as Twitter feeds, to create ways to collect the data he needed. That is, he improvised to fill in the gaps where the existing technologies did not enable him to accomplish what he needed to do. In doing so he was not strictly following the existing categories of data that the manufacturers of existing products or the Quantified Self (QS) Movement had designed and used. Instead his approach created new categories and new meanings. With his technological and design skills Chris was able to surpass, evade and expand the categories that conventional self-tracking technologies and the most established self-tracking community – QS – had established.

Chris's case is exceptional, yet it is mirrored in the improvisatory modes of self-tracking some everyday users also engage in. For example, Sarah met David, a writer, in a Melbourne bar to discuss his self-tracking. Exercise was part of David's life and included cycling to work through the city as well as more ambitious weekend rides. He and his partner had been tracking their everyday activity using Jawbone UP wristbands like ours, but did not share their data. David (also discussed in Pink et al. 2018) had learned to live with his wearable and to make meaning from its data by improvising to gain the outputs he wanted with little regard for what he believed the technology was designed to do. As he explained:

> When I first got it [the wearable] I was annoyed that it didn't pick up cycling, I was like, what you mean I just cycled all that and … so now I've started doing now is putting it in my pocket when I'm cycling, my jeans pocket, so when I'm cycling it measures the movement … if I remember I put it in my pocket, and you don't get too many steps but … even though I know that I'm doing it, I still want it to know.

This did not provide an accurate representation of David's exercise, since he was interested in registering steps rather than conforming to the process of telling the app that he was cycling so that it could measure aspects of that activity:

> You can [tell the app you are cycling] but it doesn't add to your steps … so like I go swimming, you can tell it you do swimming and stuff but I just think it … you know that they collect that data, but I don't get any reward for that … I've stopped telling it I was going for swims, because I thought, well why should I tell you, you don't care.

David's improvisatory uses of his wearable bring us back to the theme of the sensory and embodied elements of self-tracking outlined above. He wished the wearable to track what he felt he was doing and to represent that in the form of steps data. Where it was impossible, in the case of swimming, he was prepared to forfeit the steps, yet he would still know that he had exercised. Therefore, the way he produced personal data was oriented towards making meaning for him, it was patched together through his improvisatory use of the app and his embodied, sensory knowing. Significantly, this mode of self-tracking resisted the categories that were anticipated by the app design and instead redesigned the way the technologies and data could have a use and be meaningful in everyday life. There is a politics and responsibility to such use, as David pointed out: 'I don't feel I have any responsibility to give them accurate data … Yeah that's a funny idea, but it's true if everybody's using it like I am then their data might just be completely compromised.'

Like Chris, David was creative and made his data meaningful in ways that mattered to him. His example reinforces the argument that self-tracking data goes beyond representing the human body in the form of what have been critically discussed as 'data doubles' – 'decorporealized and decontextualized bodies—hybrid composites of information' which 'are intended to encourage people to act in certain ways' (Ruckenstein 2014: 4). David did not do what he believed the technology or app 'wanted' them to do, and he certainly did not do so in ways that would simply enable behaviour-change initiatives to impact on him. Rather, both he and Chris improvised to engage self-tracking technologies for their own purposes.

Methodologies for researching the temporalities of self-tracking

In order to write this book we studied the users, designers and marketing narratives of self-tracking technologies as well as the technologies themselves and the data produced with them. These are a mix of different categories of people and things from the past, present and future – users, designers technologies, narratives, visualizations and all the invisible experiential phenomena and feelings they are co-implicated with. In the remainder of this chapter we discuss how we came to know about their worlds, and in doing so we offer readers a set of methods that have been tailored to understand the complexities and temporalities of self-tracking.

Anusas and Harkness propose a version of anthropology *with* design, whereby anthropology becomes 'a line of enquiry that can *weave in with* the lives of others, rather than a discipline that has to encounter a socially encapsulated other' (2016: 57). While our research did not entail research *with* design in the sense of being in a particular making process, which is what Anusas and Harkness describe, neither is our work an academic study *of* design since our research collaborations have been with designers, and we seek to re-imagine the kinds of futures that technology design might respond to. Moreover, while a good number of the participants in our research were everyday users of self-tracking technologies, others were technology designers, or veteran users and leaders in the QS Movement themselves. At times, this even became a mode of participating in something that felt more like a collective questioning about what self-tracking means in the present and what is next in self-tracking technology design.

Starting with ourselves

We started our project with the three-month auto-ethnographic experiment discussed in the Prologue to this book, as part of our commitment to being reflexive ethnographers (Clifford and Marcus 1986) and participants in our own research. Our auto-ethnographic exercises positioned us in ways that enabled us to engage empathetically with other participants' experiences as well as understanding ourselves, our personal exercise trajectories and perceptions of our health and well-being, and our own sensory and emotional experiences as equally part of the field of users whom we sought to understand. Our auto-ethnography, moreover, enabled us to think conceptually about our own and participants' experiences and imaginations in invoking the sensoriality of embodied and spatial experience; the anticipatory modes of the possible; and the improvisatory activities through which we found our ways.

Our team approach represents what might be called collaborative auto-ethnography, which, as defined by Chang, Ngunjiri and Hernandez (2013), responds to and goes beyond more conventional inwardly focusing forms on ethnography. Drawing on this definition Morgan and Pink have discussed how collaborative auto-ethnography can direct 'analysis of self-inquiry toward broader cultural understanding and shared meaning-making'. They describe how in their shared research process 'ongoing critical dialogue between the authors (and other team members) enabled us to apply to our analysis insights gained from other research, disciplinary, literature, and professional contexts and provided a way in which to together understand the ways that Morgan learned through her autoethnographic apprenticeship' (Morgan and Pink 2017: 4). Our collaborative auto-ethnography developed as an often uncommented on and not discussed mode of sharing personal data, although it required us all to participate in order for it be possible. Therefore, rather than standing for a deep form of shared reflexivity (although we did to some extent discuss our experiences) this collective activity and our auto-ethnographic experiences became connected to our research and analytical process both as an empirical research technique and tool, and because they were deeply interwoven with the themes that emerged from the research as a tool for generating conceptual thought.

Seeking the past of self-tracking

Researching the past of something that was previously unknown requires methods that do not simply trace this phenomenon back into 'its' past. Instead, they require the researcher to become immersed in questions about and the historical traces of societies, ideas, practices and technologies, in the lives and the initiatives of pioneering individuals and in processes of scientific discovery. By entering these worlds where the devices used today remain part of an unknown and uncertain future, that could not possibly be imagined, we are able to gain a sense of the societal, cultural and technological trajectories that precede the experiential and imagined present and futures that we are now seeking to comprehend. In this sense there is not a past, present and future of self-tracking for us to connect. This raises the question of how we might know the past in ways that are ethnographically relevant – by which we do not ask how to do an *ethnography of* the past but rather of how to delve into the past, alongside and in ways that become entangled with an ethnography of the present and of imagined futures.

The point of departure for the historically driven analysis in Chapter 3 is derived largely from a combination of the words of Justjeepin (quoted in the Prologue) and our auto-ethnographic experiment. The question that engaged us concerned the issue of what we could see and what we could believe based upon the information being generated by the Jawbone UP wristband and app, which we had incorporated into our daily lives. The Jawbone worked like a mirror that produced a reflection of ourselves, but it did so by providing us with a slightly different perspective upon our bodies than we experienced phenomenologically. At the same time, however, it created what we perceived to be distortions in its reflections of us (the same problem Justjeepin complained about), like the bent mirrors in a house of mirrors at an amusement park. We apparently had a clear set of expectations of a how a mirror should work and what constituted an acceptable form of reflection from it. The questions were: where did these culturally bound understandings come from? How had we learned to mirror ourselves? And how did we learn what to expect from a mirror?

These may seem like rather banal questions. But at some point in time we guessed that the mirror must have been not only a new technology but perhaps even an innovative and exciting form of technology. This set us on the trail of the cultural history of the mirror, and repeated trips to the library and academic journals to understand how the technology of the mirror developed and how different forms of signification could have been attached to it at different periods in time. Our work led us to the seventeenth century, a juncture in time which other scholars have described as a 'century of ocular revolution' (Snyder 2015). We explain what Laura Snyder means by this in more detail in Chapter 3.

At the same time that we were digging into the cultural history of the mirror, Tom was involved in a second research project, concerning the cultural economy of heritage sites in Sweden, and doing fieldwork at Skokloster Castle, outside of Stockholm. Skokloster is one of the best preserved baroque-style castles left in Europe. It is the home to a vast intact collection of weapons and instruments of the time. Tom decided to take advantage of his time in Skokloster Castle to pose new questions to what he saw and observed, not about heritage and economics, but about body monitoring. Clearly, no one in the seventeenth century spoke about data in the way we do today in relation to processes of digitalization, but perhaps it was possible to use the castle as an empirical site to better understand how people in the seventeenth century were coming to re-think and re-understand what it meant to see, and to make observations about themselves and the world around them. Viewing the castle in this light, and analysing it against the background of knowledge we had procured about the cultural history of mirrors and of seeing, made the castle ethnographically powerful. What emerged was a story that no guides at the castle told and that involved artefacts and pieces of material culture that guides and visitors ignored, or just did not see because they seemed so mundane from today's perspective. But one of the most important insights from this work was that, without the cultural knowledge and experiences that still resonated from the castle's seventeenth-century past, very little of what people do today with digital monitoring apps would make sense. The castle, in short, allowed us to use ethnographic observations made there to provide depth to our understanding of how people worked with digital technologies of body monitoring and data collection in the present.

Ethnographies with users

Our ethnographic approach to everyday life involves understanding the present as always being an articulation of uniquely configured and contingent circumstances, which continually slips over into the past as a new present emerges. Many of the self-trackers who participated in our research did not belong to a community of self-trackers, such as the QS Movement; we needed to meet them alone, in intensive encounters (Pink and Morgan 2013). These encounters were in places generally selected because they were convenient to the participants, including: at cafés near to where they worked, at their homes, by Skype or at our universities. Here we were concerned with how participants experienced and made everyday self-tracking meaningful and were particularly attentive to how they improvised with technologies and data to achieve this as 'users' or, in the case of those responsible for designing self-tracking technologies, as 'user-designers'. We were also concerned with how participants imagined their possible future selves and technologies through their experiences, anxieties and aspirations relating to self-tracking and used our encounters with people and their technologies to probe how they might imagine future possibilities. In particular, we were interested in how they envisaged their future health, data privacy and security and the power relations this assumed, and their hopes for the technologies they would use in the future.

In our research with these participants we used video ethnography and sensory ethnography techniques (Pink 2013; 2015), in face-to-face and online encounters. We wanted to understand not just what people said about self-tracking technologies but what they did with them. We asked participants to show us their use and in some cases also to teach us how to use the devices and apps, whenever possible video recording these performances. For example, in Australia, when Sarah met Christof in her university building he opened his mediation app and showed her how he monitored his response by clipping a device on his ear. When she met David at his home he walked her through his morning routine of weighing himself and inputting his data to the platform where his Fitbit data was automatically shown. David and Sarah discussed why he did not have scales that could upload the data for him, and shortly after their meeting he bought some. When Josefine showed Vaike her running app, she pretended that she was lying on her sofa watching TV and when the commercials came on she re-enacted her routine of browsing through her iPad and scrolling through different kinds of social media, news and self-tracking apps. We also used GoPro video techniques, asking self-tracking cyclists to wear a camera on their helmet, to record their ride and then discuss this video in an interview with a researcher (Pink et al. 2017). Other interviews were also performed over Skype. When Vaike got in contact with Jens he wanted to show how his smartphone had 'enslaved' him, and during the Skype interview he was at home and could easily show with props from different rooms how his devices 'forced' him to walk some extra 100 steps at night before he went to bed to come up to the goals set in the app and where he did that to not disturb the rest of his family.

We sought to bring to the fore not just what people said about their uses of self-tracking but to invite them to reflect on these experiences, and in doing so to use this self-knowledge as a prompt and basis through which to consider and imagine futures. Therefore, our encounters with participants followed a guide which began with a consideration of the stories through which they had become self-trackers, how the devices fitted into their lives and what they imagined for the future, including discussing scenarios that are reported in media, including examples such as covering both hopes and fears relating to how health insurance companies might use their data and how they felt about

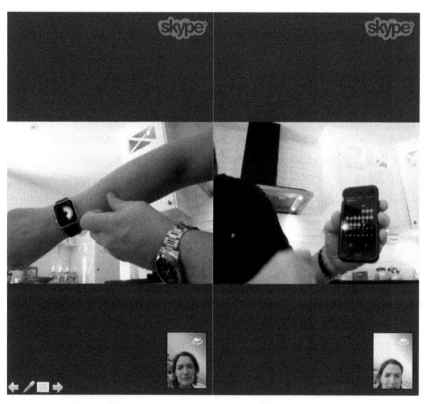

Figure 2.1 Jens shows Vaike, over Skype, how he uses his self-tracking app in his home. Screenshot: Vaike Fors.

the possibilities of types of surveillance in the present and the consequences this might have in the future. Such reflections inspired some participants to make changes: David purchased a new wireless weighing scale, and another participant, who felt uncomfortable about the idea of surveillance after our encounter, actually gave up tracking.

Our ethnographic research with users encompassed both committed and longer term self-trackers and people who had stopped tracking themselves after a short while. We also interviewed very experienced and influential self-trackers, who we call 'veterans', to better understand how they imagined what will happen next and where self-tracking is heading now that the hype of the first generation of digital tracking devices is over.

Ethnographies with devices and systems

Despite their claims to become part of people's lives and bodies – making friends with their users, as it were – self-tracking apps and devices are comparatively closed systems that do not easily lend themselves to critical inquiry. This creates certain methodological challenges since the algorithmically driven analysis and visualization of personal data, around which these devices and systems revolve, are structured by how their makers imagine the bodies and everyday lives of users. Furthermore, these devices and systems are often interconnected through various forms of APIs (application programming interfaces), such as the Apple HealthKit or Google Fit, that allow apps and devices to become part of a larger ecosystem where personal data can be transferred, translated, combined and interpreted. Although these backstage parts of self-tracking devices and apps might be regarded as singularly unexciting on the surface, they are indeed crucial for understanding how 'behind-the-scenes decisions' are made and how certain forms of data and engagements with data become encouraged through the databases and the code that make devices and apps work together (Star 2002). Not only do self-tracking APIs provide 'invisible layers of control and access' that brings about certain 'social orderings' (Star 2002), but they also limit and guide design processes in certain directions by allowing access to a larger data ecosystem on the condition that only certain data types are permitted to flow between devices (see also Van Dijck and Poell 2016). Our own empirical research has approached the visions, values and imaginaries that are built into self-tracking devices and systems drawing on digital ethnography (Pink et al. 2016), critical app studies (Light, Burgess and Duguay 2018) and reverse engineering (Gehl 2014). Such an approach has led us to engage with and interview people who design and market self-tracking devices, make participant observations at biohacking events, and to perform content analyses of an array of promotional and instructional materials, such as sales pitches, blog posts and public presentations of self-tracking technologies. Together, these methodologies allowed us to grasp the assumptions that are built into these technologies as sociocultural products underpinned by their makers' ideas, assumptions and agendas, while at the same time exploring the tensions between the technologically possible and how these possibilities are explained to potential users (see also Adams and Thompson 2016). In our studies, we have focused on the interpretive repertoire employed when the imagined value and function of self-tracking devices and systems are described and how they relate to and result from broader social and cultural processes (Berg 2017; Boztepe and Berg forthcoming). In our interviews and observations, we focused specifically on how underlying ideas and assumptions that refer to tacit, sensory, habitual and seemingly mundane elements of everyday life have influenced the product development process (Fors, Berg and Pink 2016) or how the body is imagined as technologically reshapable (Berg, Fors and Eriksson 2016). Engaging with questions of how and why these technologies should make sense and become meaningful for users as well as questions of why designers and marketing people imagine these to be valid assumptions has allowed us to approach what is going on 'under the hood' from the outside and from where these devices and systems are situated in the world. Engaging with the materials this way involves, as Gillespie (2014) suggests, looking closer at how these devices and systems make data 'algorithm ready' and follow certain criteria to determine which data are thought of as relevant as well as how calculated publics are produced through, for instance, data doubles (Ruckenstein 2014) and algorithmic identities (Cheney-Lippold 2011). Interrogating these processes and procedures allows us to understand how algorithms and data work in specific ways, and how they become part of the cultural forms of our current information ecosystem (Striphas 2015) and produce imaginable futures. As our discussion of the findings of these studies shows in Chapter 4, we found that by only allowing certain forms of data and metrics to count as such, self-tracking devices and systems rely on imaginaries where only ideal (and perhaps even non-existent) bodies and selves can fit, thus, often contrary to the idea behind these technologies, allowing for imaginative and creative sense-making practices among everyday users (as further discussed in Chapter 5).

Participant observations and workshops

During the life of the project we actively looked for opportunities to interact with different kinds of self-tracking communities and learn together with them during conferences and workshops. We also organized a design futures workshop with invited experienced self-trackers, developers and researchers. We participated as researchers in a biohacking conference in Helsinki, where we also were part of a 'upgraded dinner', a biohacking cooking class where we got in contact with the biohacking forerunners in Finland and could ask about how they imagined what was around the corner in this community. We also proposed and organized a workshop for the Quantified Self conference in Amsterdam in 2017.

By naming the workshop 'Future Learning with Digital Health Service Design', we wanted to disrupt current design systems of self-tracking and health services by re-thinking such devices as future tools for *learning* instead of as tools for *behavioural change*.

In Chapter 1 we discussed how researchers and participants collaborated in a Design Futures workshop to explore together how the 'what next' of self-tracking technologies might be experienced. This mode of coming together to imagine the future of personal data characterized our research process throughout. Our ethnographic, workshop-based and historical fieldwork took us into the lives of past, present and future self-trackers through novel collaborative and empathetic research techniques through which we sought to understand a series of differently situated experiences of what it must feel like to live with personal data.

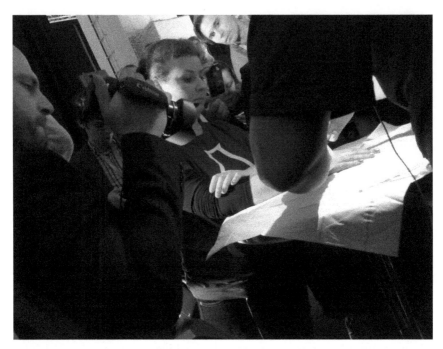

Figure 2.2 Participant observations by Martin at the Biohacker Summit in Helsinki 2015. Photo: Vaike Fors.

The workshop is a core research and exploratory activity in the context of design practice, yet in academic ethnographic disciplines it has tended to be little used. This is partly because conventional workshop methods are often too rigid for the exploratory nature of academic research (Berg and Fors 2017). However, recently, as design anthropological and ethnographic approaches become increasingly popular, the workshop is emerging in new theoretical, methodological and practical forms as a core technique for the generation of new ways of knowing, imagining and sharing activities and experiences (Akama, Pink and Sumartojo 2018). This makes the newly constituted workshop an ideal context through which to investigate, bring to the surface, share and generate empathetic sentiments around sensory and embodied experience.

Summing up

In this chapter we have brought together the theoretical, conceptual, thematic and methodological strands of our research. These are interwoven throughout this book, always in dialogue and always relational to each other. The questions, theory and method that frame our discussions are framed through a processual understanding of the environment, imagination and learning which calls for the temporal approach that we have taken. Our ways of knowing about self-tracking as part of our past, present and future have emerged through encounters with texts, artefacts, technologies, users, developers, designers, media and data. In these encounters, our analysis and our writing, likewise we understand our own encounters with everyday environments, people and technologies, our imaginations as researchers and the modes through which we learn to be equally incremental, processual and open, to be continuing rather than ending. We invite readers to engage with reading this book on the same terms, that is by understanding themselves as equally part of a continually changing environment where encounters with the experiences of researchers and research participants are not fixed, and where we do not intend to have a single impact on readers. Rather, we wish our readers to join us in opening up the discussion about self-tracking and personal data.

3

Ubiquitous Monitoring Technologies in Historical Perspective

Both the people in Australia and Sweden who participated in our research and ourselves as researchers had come to take for granted that we can measure ourselves, our daily activities and the things that we encountered in them. However, the processes through which our ability to understand our bodies as quantifiable came about as part of the history of science, technology and innovation. In this chapter we situate self-tracking technologies as part of our worlds by asking what we might learn from historical examples of technologies that monitor or measure the human body and have become enduringly ubiquitous in everyday life. Through an analysis of historical written accounts, sites and reported events of technological and scientific innovation and use, we investigate how and why certain technologies of human measurement have become ubiquitous in our lives. We examine what they have enabled people and societies to know, how visualization and sensory ways of knowing have been implicated in their design and use, and how they have impacted on human perception of the spatiality of everyday worlds. In developing a historical account, however, we wish to disturb the idea that self-tracking technologies themselves have a 'history'. Instead, we consider how the human experiences, activities and practices associated with historical technologies of body monitoring and measurement have become culturally embedded.

In what follows we first discuss early forms of scientific quantification, followed by examples of three technologies: the weight scale, the mirror and the X-ray. These are not necessarily the precursors of self-tracking, but they are ubiquitous everyday body technologies whose trajectories help us to understand how other self-tracking technologies and personal data are becoming part of our everyday environments, activities, experiences, anxieties and hopes.

Early meanings of data

According to the *Oxford English Dictionary*, the use of the term data as denoting numbers that are 'typically collected together for reference, analysis, or calculation' stretches back to the seventeenth century.[1] This understanding of data as 'something given or granted; something known or assumed as fact' is still widely assumed. Although such an understanding of data as pre-analytical entities works as a semantic foundation for how the concept is used, the meaning of the term data has changed over the years. In his exploration of conceptual development of the term data, Rosenberg (2013) shows that it is not only linked to societal changes and the development of modern understandings of knowledge but also that it played an important role in opening up a 'conceptual space' for modern information technology. The term data gained an increased popularity from the middle of the twentieth century onwards due its importance for contexts of computing where data came to denote 'quantities, characters, or symbols on which operations are performed by a computer, considered collectively' (36). In contrast to the use of data as something given (due to its roots in the Latin verb *dare*, 'to give'), present-day uses of the term data often refer to something that is taken or extracted (thus meaning *capta*, from the Latin word *capere*, 'to take'). Indeed, it seems that contemporary uses of the term data build on both of these concepts: data are taken or extracted from something given or factual. This duality should be understood in light of Rosenberg's observation that the semantic function of the term data is 'specifically rhetorical' since, when compared to facts or evidence, for instance, data stands out as rarely being questioned or regarded as theory-laden. Rosenberg explains this further and argues that data means 'that which is given prior to an argument' (36), and for that reason it has remained an outlier in spite of the fundamentally important and game-changing epistemological developments over the last couple of centuries. Curiously, Rosenberg adds, 'the preexisting semantic structure of the term "data" made it especially flexible in these shifting epistemological and semantic contexts. Without changing meaning, during the eighteenth century data changed connotation. It went from being reflexively associated with those things that are outside of any possible process of discovery to being the very paradigm of what one seeks through experiment and observation' (36).

Measuring the body

The process of scientific study that led to early forms of quantification of the human body dates back to the so-called 'Chemical Revolution' in the mid- to late eighteenth century in which scholars sought to understand – and focused on measuring – the chemistry of our bodies, through a stringent reliance on quantitative methods. During this period a new vocabulary about 'nutrition' and 'metabolism' began to take form. One of the earliest systematic studies in the young field of nutrition came from experiments conducted in 1746 by James Lind, a ship's surgeon in the British Navy who strove to understand the causes of, and possible cures for, scurvy amongst sailors (Carpenter 2003: 643). At the time, sailors were commonly given vinegar or diluted forms of sulphuric acid as a cure for scurvy, but this simply did not work. Lind initiated a controlled test with twelve sailors suffering from scurvy, half of them were given vinegar and half of them a diet of lemons and citrus fruit. Those receiving the lemons recovered, while those receiving vinegar did not. This was not a new discovery, since it had been known for over two hundred years that citrus fruit could cure scurvy. However, the fruit went mouldy on longer sea journeys so the Navy, believing that the key curative ingredient was sulphuric acid (which could be stored without moulding), had equipped ship's doctors with sulphuric acid without ever testing to see if this was the key ingredient. Lind therefore contributed one of the first controlled clinical tests and methods of data collection in the field of nutrition, and started an expansive field of scholars striving to use systematic study and quantitative methods to understand nutrition (Carpenter 2003).

During the following century a scientific race developed to understand how the body could be measured in different ways. At this time the concept of 'the calorie' became increasingly important, as French scholars derived different ways to define the calorie in relation to human energy needs. The difficulty was coming to an agreement on the best way of understanding how the energy in the foods we eat could be calculated and described in a singular, standardized unit, which took the better part of a century. The introduction of the term in the American vocabulary is attributed to an article written by Atwater in 1887, which was then further disseminated by the USDA Farmer's Bulletin (Hargrove 2006: 2960). As a consequence, ordinary people had a highly abstract concept to use when speaking about how much energy they were putting into their bodies and how much they were expending in relation to their physical activity.

However, it was one thing to begin to think more stringently about how the body could be measured, it was quite another thing for ordinary people to begin to think that they could (or should) do this themselves. From the late nineteenth century and through the twentieth century the use of self-help books and the question of developing new forms of self-actualization played a role, focusing on topics ranging from psychoanalysis, sexual therapy, diet and weight loss to the advocation of an endless array of training and fitness programmes (Starker 1989). The weight scale, to which we now turn our attention, was implicated in this as a measuring technology.

The weight scale is both currently part of self-tracking practices and embedded in the cultural histories of much of the world. Indeed, Crawford, Lingel and Karppi (2015), who compare contemporary wearables with a 'historical predecessor' of self-tracking technologies, the weight scale, note that, 'Since the late 19th century … [weight scales have] become one of the most pervasive and familiar self-monitoring technologies.' The weight scales of the nineteenth century initially became available in places such as public railway stations, and bathroom scales became increasingly prevalent in the home in the first decades of the twentieth century. However, as they moved from the public domain into the privacy of the home there was an uncertainty as to what the realm of technological possibilities this newly domesticized instrument could offer. One bathroom scale, called the 'health-o-meter', for example, promised users in a sales advertisement that they could take off weight 'where desired'. To help them achieve this goal it came equipped with a second form of technology – a programme written by physicians that promised a woman the ability to 'mould your figure to your wishes'.[2] The expectations of what a bathroom scale could accomplish were, at this time, still in the process of being calibrated to realistically align with its actual potential.

Indeed, the history of the weight scale provides a useful historical comparison to the ubiquity of contemporary self-tracking technologies since, as Crawford, Lingel and Karppi note, 'In many ways, the weight scale offers us a powerful example of how a monitoring device can move through different spaces: from the doctor's office to public squares and streets, and eventually into the home' (2015: 481). Their analysis revealed that, rather than being only about managing one's weight, monitoring weight through use of the bathroom scales had, since the 1890s, been associated with being 'a powerful form of self-knowledge' (483). They suggest that 'This connection between knowing one's weight data and self-knowledge at a deeper level continued as the weight scale moved from public space to the domestic sphere, and continues today, where value and self-worth can be attached to the number of pounds weighed.' They argue that 'With the emergence of wearable self-tracking devices, remarkably similar claims appear: self-tracking will lead to self-knowledge' (483). However, as Crawford and colleagues point out, the important difference between the historical weight scale and contemporary wearables is that the scale reported data directly back to the user without aggregating or sharing it, while the wearable data is shared and used by third parties.

Glass, mirrors and technologies of seeing the body

Mirrors have long been involved in the social organization of how bodies and selves are understood. Based in medieval Christian traditions, mirrors played a central role in the development of the significance of self-consciousness in the West, through the mirror's reflection the self became understood through *appearance* (Melchoir-Bonnet 2001). And the mirror is the first technological instrument which we are exposed to as children and which opens to us that which we cannot see – our own faces, our eyes, our smiles, ourselves. It is the very first instrument by which we come to compare ourselves to others, and which allows us to think that we see ourselves as others do. It is through the technology of the mirror that the ballet dancer strives to perfect their movements and earn a place in a dance company. And it is the technology in relation to which millions of teenagers have measured their bodies as they have lifted weights, performed aerobics, applied make-up and judged the fit of clothing.

The next part of this chapter addresses this question through a historical perspective to uncover and illuminate the processes of cultural change and technology design through which it has become possible for the body to be viewed from beyond the limits of our internal interpretations of how our bodies feel. To do this we have selected, as an example from the seventeenth century, Skokloster Castle, Sweden, as a location and moment in history through which to explore the emergence of technologies of vision.[3] The seventeenth century is interesting due to the fact that it is a period of time which other scholars have referred to as 'a century of ocular revolution' (Snyder 2015), and some regard it as representing a turn towards ocularcentrism that was to endure in modern Western societies. Skokloster is interesting in this case as it provides us with a particular physical point in which to anchor and empirically contextualize our discussion. Our goal here is to situate the castle's trajectory in relation to the development of technologies of vision in Europe during this period. As we argue, the seventeenth century is particularly interesting for our analysis because it was during this period that Europeans came to successively problematize and rethink what it meant to see: to see the world around them and to see, understand and gain new perspectives on themselves (see Snyder 2015). Skokloster is an ideal example through which to examine the implications of this since it provides us with a concrete context in which to peer into the technologies of the seventeenth century, while offering us a unique intact collection and inventory of the cutting-edge technologies of the period.

Skokloster Castle: Seventeenth-century technologies for knowing the body

Skokloster Castle in Sweden (Figure 3.1) was built between 1654 and 1676 by Baron Carl Gustaf Wrangel, who had established a reputation for himself as a highly successful military leader in the Thirty Years War in which Sweden rose in military prominence and temporarily made large land gains in central Europe. Over the course of his career Wrangel accrued such titles as field marshal, Lord High Admiral of Sweden and governor-general of Swedish Pomerania. His rise in rank occurred at a time in history when it became increasingly important for men of power and position to be able to manifest their status through the possessions they owned, and particularly to the extent that those possessions attested to their owner's worldliness and refined understanding of the arts, sciences and literature of the day. Against this

Figure 3.1 Skokloster Castle, Sweden. Photo: Tom O'Dell.

background Wrangel became a collector of furniture, art, books, weapons and the most refined instruments and tools of his day (Boström 1975: 5). To house his collection and create a summer residence for his family, he began the construction of Skokloster Castle in 1654 on the shores of Lake Mälaren to the west of Stockholm. As construction proceeded he assembled his collections there. Paintings were hung and furniture was moved in gradually as room after room was completed. Wrangel died in 1676 and his oldest daughter Margareta Juliana converted Skokloster Castle into an entailed estate in 1701, which effectively forbade the selling, giving away or transference via inheritance of any of the castle's belongings. While the furniture, art and contents of many European castles were sold off over the centuries to finance their upkeep, Skokloster remained intact. It therefore offers the contemporary world a unique view of how the material and technological culture of Europe's elite was organized centuries ago. Indeed, entering Skokloster Castle is perhaps the closest one can come to time travel, and in this sense brings us close up to the technologies available at the time. With the exception of the administrative offices for the staff that work in the museum at Skokloster, the castle is unheated and lacks electricity. Winter temperatures dip well below freezing indoors as well as outdoors.

One of the most important developing technologies of the time can be found throughout the castle, but it seems so trivial today that guides never mention it in tours, and tourists hardly notice it. It is glass. In contemporary society we take glass for granted and are indeed surrounded by it, from the disposable packaging used for bottling soft drinks to the large storefront windows that line our town and city streets. However, considering glass as part of a history of technology design helps us to look at it differently: artisans struggled for centuries to perfect the processes involved in the production of glass. Different mixtures of sands, ashes and minerals produced glass that was tinted in various shades of green, blue, yellow and brown, but finding the right balance to make clear colourless glass was difficult, as was developing the skills and techniques to blow glass that was devoid of bubbles and ripples, or larger panes of flat glass. In the mid-seventeenth century, when the construction of Skokloster was initiated, these were all aspects of glassmaking that artisans were still struggling to perfect.

Figure 3.2 The large glass windows in the Red Bedchamber at Skokloster enable the flow of light into the room. Photo: Tom O'Dell.

In the seventeenth century, with no electricity, maximizing daylight was a necessity, and the panes of glass needed to fill the castle's dozens of enormous windows were not only a luxury of the most spectacular kind but also marked the beginning of a technological revolution. Wrangel incorporated glass into the construction of his home in ways that only the absolutely wealthiest in Europe could. Skokloster's windows were made of over 7,500 panes of glass and represented the cutting edge of illuminative technology at the time. Glass allowed for the flow of light into interiors and thus created a technological framework for the orchestration of the social space of the home as well as framing the outside world for those standing within (Figure 3.2). The placement of sitting groups and furniture arrangements followed the dictates of the window's illuminative power – as well as the placing of the fireplace, which provided both warmth and a source of illumination when the sun faded – and can be seen in the inner walls of Skokloster where tapestries and canvases were hung. Moreover, the light from the castle's windows revealed new ways to see and frame bodies.

Revising the human body

The emergence of such technologies of vision and the artistic and scientific pursuits that they became implicated in is part of what historians of the visual have referred to as a move towards an ocularcentrism, which valued scientific knowledge that was grounded in empirical observation rather than philosophical speculation or attention to the wider range of sensory knowledge. Yet, as the anthropologist Ingold has warned, we should be wary of such assumptions that the discourse of vision really dominated the ways in which people experienced and felt their worlds, since without a real understanding of how 'seeing in *actual practice*, rather than as imagined by philosophers' (Ingold 2000: 286) we must defer any claims that this moment was a step in the making of an ocularcentric or 'visualist' (Fabian 1983) modern Western culture. Indeed, rather than assuming that these new technologies impacted culture and shifted the ways people understood their worlds, it is more coherent with our project in this book and our interpretation of how self-tracking technologies and data visualization play a part in contemporary everyday lives to rethink the emerging technologies of vision of the seventeenth century beyond a solutionism paradigm, which sees technologies as solving particular problems that society is seen as being confronted by (Morozov 2013), towards the question of what they made possible. Indeed, as we detail next, the case of Skokloster is interesting in this sense. Before returning to Wrangel, however, we discuss further how the emerging glass technologies of this period began to make possible new ways of seeing and understanding the world. As Laura Snyder puts it, they 'allowed that there was more to nature than meets the naked eye, since lenses, and other optical instruments, could help us see a part of nature that was otherwise hidden'. She goes on to argue that, 'For the first time the question of *how* we see assumed a central place in science, and what it meant, precisely, to *see* was radically reconceived. And in the midst of this upheaval of thought, science and art came together … to shed light on what it really meant to see the world' (Snyder 2015: 7f.).

The new possibilities for seeing can be attributed to a dramatic expansion in the development and refinement of glass lenses, as new techniques for polishing and making convex and concave forms of glass developed. This led to a new technological innovation: the development of the telescope (due to new understandings of how concave and convex lenses could be combined to magnify sight) which was patented in 1608, in the Netherlands. A year later, telescopes were popping up in shops in Paris, Milan and London. Galileo refined the technique further to produce telescopes in 1610 that could magnify images twenty to thirty times in size, and which were fitted with apertures to better control the flow of light through the instrument, and in the same year he inverted this technology to develop the microscope (61). It suddenly became apparent that much of the world was not as it had first appeared: the water people drank was not pure and clear, but full of slithering organisms; household flies, it was discovered, had more eyes than one could imagine; and the moon wasn't flat but completely full of mountains and topographical irregularities (9).

The arts and sciences were co-implicated in this new way of seeing, scientists were educated in art and artists were increasingly called upon to represent nature in ways that were more scientifically true than their predecessors had depicted. This was supported particularly through another glass-based technological advance, in the form of the camera obscura, which opened the way for a new understanding of what was actually seen by the eye. The camera obscura worked like a pinhole camera but without film. Light entered through a small hole and was reflected upside-down and inverted on the top of the camera or on another surface, such as a wall or canvas. Convex lenses and mirrors were added to the camera obscura, which made the images they projected sharper while simultaneously amplifying the strength of the colours, hues and shadows that they projected (127ff.). As a result, artists began to experiment with different lenses that allowed them to study the lighting of scenes in ways they had not been able to do previously. Indeed, the way in which the camera obscura intensified colours and inverted images raised questions about what the eye actually could see – while also providing artists with the potential to be more accurate in their painting than ever before (Crary 1992: 33). Working in this spirit of accuracy, portrait, landscape and still-life artists strove for new levels of precision and honesty to the ephemeral and ever-shifting dance between light, colour and shadows that were the basis of seeing (Ambjörnsson 2016). In the pursuit of trying to learn the truth about nature and that which lay beyond the capabilities of the naked eye, artists engaged their subjects with a new fervour of portraying surfaces that went deeper than the surface. With the help of mathematics, geometry and inventions such as the camera obscura, they fine honed their understandings of perspective and how perspectives could be better portrayed on canvas.

This had implications for the ways that what we might think of as the personal data of the seventeenth century could be visualized. At Skokloster, Wrangel lined the walls of his home with hundreds of oil paintings dating from the early fifteenth century onward that, when seen from today's perspective, constitute a genealogy of representation – at the juncture of art and science – that strove in the direction of trying to see, study and understand the world through more accurate forms of representation. The struggle to come to grips with seeing the world and the body 'as it really was', and the issue of portraying perspectives and fine tuning the degree to which oils on canvas could portray the world as accurately as possible is well illustrated by two portraits of Wrangel himself: one of him as a child (Figure 3.3), painted in 1619, and the other of him as an adult on the battlefield from 1652 (Figure 3.4). The latter depicts Wrangel in a way that seems close to 3D correctness (the horse, Wrangel and the battlefield are aligned in a clear singular perspective). The earlier portrait of

Figure 3.3 Portrait of Carl Gustaf Wrangel as a child, 1619. Belonging to the collection of Skokloster Castle, inventory number 2148.

him as a child in contrast is a kaleidoscope of perspectives and planes. Wrangel is presented from one perspective, the table to his left is flattened and tilted upward in another perspective. He is holding a hat, but the width of the hat seems to make it impossible to hold, and the hand holding it is from an angle that would be impossible to achieve. The pillar behind him points in a different direction to the table in front of him, and the brush on the table assumes yet another angle than the table itself.

Walking through Skokloster Castle, one also encounters a world of kings, queens, admirals, barons, captains, historic battles and inspiring landscapes, as well as still lifes and studies of the faces of unknown subjects that span this distance in understanding perspective and how perspectives could be worked to produce 'truer and truer' renderings of reality and the world as it

Figure 3.4 Portrait of Carl Gustaf Wrangel on a horse, David Klöcker Ehrenstrahl, 1652. Belonging to the collection of Skokloster Castle, inventory number 698.

was. The 1652 painting by David Klöcker Ehrenstrahl, which depicts Wrangel on horseback, provides an example of what such visualizations could suggest. Wrangel's head is turned to the right, he stares straight at the viewer while his body and the horse he sits on are facing the right side of the painting. Behind Wrangel lies a dark battle-bitten landscape with fire and smoke billowing into the air. Wrangel has his sword drawn in his right hand, horizontally positioned between himself and the viewer, with a pistol tucked in under his saddle. His chest is protected with breast armour, but otherwise he is dressed in gold and white satins, wearing a dark hat with plumage of large white and blue feathers. Behind him, in the upper-left corner of the painting, are three large billowing flags in shades of blue, yellow and white, bearing images of lions and crowns.

Wrangel is here depicted as a man of the world, a man of knowledge and a warrior. He is confident, strong and unflinching. But what is perhaps most significant is that his horse is rearing up on its back legs, since this is a compositional position that had always been reserved for kings and royalty. The painting is, indeed, one of the first and earliest pieces of work depicting a non-royal in this way in the Swedish context. Wrangel was in fact very close to the Swedish king and had been given the estate of Skokloster as a reward for his service and loyalty. Like many kings of his time, Wrangel had his own 'artist of the court', David Klöcker Ehrenstrahl, whom he enlisted over and over again to produce works for his estates.[4]

The significance of this particular painting both in its time, and for our interest in the question of how otherwise invisible personal information was visualized historically, lies in how it depicts that which the naked eye could not see in 'real life': the alignment of Wrangel with the position of kings. The pose Ehrenstrahl rendered, with the rearing horse and symbolic association with royalty, is no accident. Wrangel and Ehrenstrahl would have undoubtedly communicated extensively on this exact composition. It speaks in part of qualities hidden under the surface of Wrangel's skin, and it moreover reveals how Wrangel could *imagine himself* in an elevated social position – as a body and inner self akin to a king. The painting itself is slightly larger than 3 metres by 3 metres in dimension, and Wrangel – as depicted in the painting – is nearly 1.8 metres tall (even though he is not standing erect but seated on a horse). It is not just that he is larger than life but also that he and his inner being are magnified and revealed to visitors to Skokloster in ways that only oil and canvas could allow. The technological advances of the seventeenth century did not simply lead to more realistic representations of bodies and landscapes but reframed them in ways that claimed to reveal more than could be seen by the naked eye. As we will argue below, contemporary self-tracking devices do something similar.

From technologies of light to mirrors

Prior to the seventeenth century, large wall-mounted glass mirrors were very rare and tended to be made of well-polished metals such as brass, copper and silver. Later, early forms of glass, such as the smaller panes that were used for windows, were tinted in shades of brown, green, blue and yellow and the mirrors made from them reflected those hues. The development of pure colourless glass required mastering the right mix of sands and ashes. But complicating the production of the mirror further was the need to develop the right techniques for handling glass as well as silvering it. The first glass mirrors were made from blown glass and were thus rounded and rather small, often no larger than a hand (Melchior-Bonnet 2001). The Venetians led the way in the seventeenth century in developing the art of blowing larger and larger balls of glass that could be punctured and spun into discs with sizes of up to 1.2 metres in diameter. These were the basis for the first large flat mirrors that came to be desired and coveted by the highest ranks of royalty in the mid-seventeenth century. For the Venetians, this was a gold mine of export revenue, and the secrets of making large flat panes of glass were held tightly. Only the king could designate who was allowed to enter and practice the trade of mirror making. Craftsmen who were lured abroad to countries such as Germany or France to practice – or worse, teach – their trade risked assassination, or having their possessions confiscated by the Crown and their families imprisoned until their return (36ff).

A central problem remained until the late seventeenth century: the size of mirrors was limited to the size that glass could be blown. Existing methods could produce a round flat glass surface of about 1.2 metres in diameter, but in the middle of this sheet of glass was the bulb that joined the glass mass that was being blown to the blowing pipe. Once the sheet of glass was cut to omit this bulb, the largest square pains were limited to approximately 61 centimetres by 61 centimetres. And it was not until the 1680s that techniques for casting large panes of glass evolved. Until then, large mirrors were made of multiple panes and were still very expensive, and as regards their owner, the larger the mirror, the more prestige it reflected.

In contrast to the large ornate portraits that embellish the castle's walls, the mirrors might seem mundane to the contemporary visitor, but for Wrangel they would have been the opposite. Indeed, in 1672, he had an inventory made of his possessions at the castle. The inventory does not include everything he owned, but it does thoroughly list his most prized possessions. On the last page of the inventory, listed with other objects he called 'instruments' are '4 large mirrors' (Figure 3.5). One of these is likely to be the one hanging in

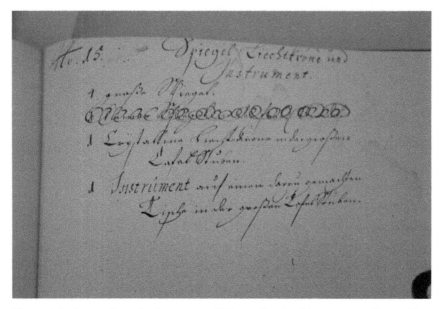

Figure 3.5 A page from the inventory of Wrangel's prized instruments. Photo: Tom O'Dell.

the baroness's drawing room which is believed to have been made sometime between 1650 and 1700 (Figure 3.6). The status the mirror would have had is reflected in its framing. Whereas the large portrait of Wrangel on his horse is framed in a rather simple gold painted wooden frame, the mirror has an intricately handcrafted frame of bronze and silver with a diamond-like jewel on top.

When purchased for the castle, the three other large mirrors in the neighbouring rooms could have cost more than ten times the amount of the large oil paintings around them (Knutsson 1987: 8). In the seventeenth and eighteenth centuries mirrors were morally loaded and different mirrors were related to different moral dispositions, in that 'The little mirror was left open to accusations of frivolity and lies, whereas the large one was said to speak the truth of a person' (Melchior-Bonnet 2001: 143). The hand mirror was a tool for personal use, grooming, dabbling and adoring the self. The large mirror, however, was framed to reflect something worthy of being seen, and the frame itself was designed to acknowledge the dignity of the glass within its perimeters.

Figure 3.6 The large mirror hanging in the baroness's drawing room at Skokloster Castle. Photo: Tom O'Dell.

The fact that these large mirrors were listed on the same page in the inventory as other 'instruments' gives a good indication of how Wrangel and the peers of his time saw and understood them. If the small mirror was a morally questionable artefact of frivolity, the large mirror was a social instrument that allowed those of rank to not only observe themselves but to observe others, *and to allow themselves to be observed by others*. The larger mirror didn't limit the gaze to a specific disjointed portion of the body (the face, the lips, the eyes) but opened the entire body to view within a larger social context. It simultaneously offered a slightly magical quality by putting the social reality before it into a slightly different perspective (revealing angles and qualities that were unavailable to the viewer's unassisted eye). The inclusion of mirrors in extravagantly decorated interiors worked as a significant social medium, heightening the ability of everyone in the room to see – and thus confirm – one another, while also testing the veracity of what the angle of their own eyes offered. Simultaneously, the technology of the large silvered panes of glass at Skokloster spoke back to the status, power and position of its hosts.

However, the mirrors at Skokloster did not stand alone, they were embedded in a larger assemblage of material culture – from the very architectural layout of the castle, its windows and the fall of light, to the organization of the objects and furnishings in the room and oil paintings that the mirrors were placed between. As Bennett has argued,

> The effects generated by assemblages are … emergent in that their ability to make something happen … is distinct from the sum of the vital force of each materiality considered alone. Each member and proto-member of the assemblage has a certain vital force, but there is also an effectivity proper to the grouping as such: an agency of the assemblage. (2010: 24)

The mirrors, like all body-monitoring technologies since them, derived their agency and ability to frame bodies (with layers of morally laden signification) from not only themselves but even via the other objects in their presence that they drew together. If large mirrors were generally understood to speak to the truths of their reflection, then the paintings and furnishings of the castle accentuated the social positions and qualities of the bodies before them. Indeed, in order to work at Skokloster, mirrors required frames that contributed to their drama and shared the aesthetic grammar of those around the portraits lining Skokloster's walls, aligning in this sense the reflected images of guests with the painted oil persona of kings, nobility and war heroes.

However, the reflection of the mirror is very often dependent upon, or subsumed in, broader forms of technological assemblages. It is, for example, interesting to note that the technology of the mirror was even often accompanied by other low technologies in the pursuit of perfection. For example, back in the 1960s and 1970s, comic books regularly included advertisements for Charles Atlas's workout programme. The advertisements included a comic strip depiction of a skinny guy and his girlfriend being bullied at the beach by a muscular jock. To add insult to injury, the woman in the comic comforted her partner by saying, 'Don't let it bother you little boy!' In the following frame, the 'little boy' takes action and orders Atlas's workout programme and soon stands in front of the mirror looking like Charles Atlas himself! Similar sorts of workout programmes (from the 'Batman Workout' to any of an array of 'learn at home', mail-order courses in martial arts) were sold to teenagers around the world in this period (and continue to be sold). They offered not only instructions in bodybuilding but even clear reference points of comparison as the technology of the mirror was coupled with the technology of the page in the workout brochure.

Thus we have seen how the sensed body is 'seen' and made visible, what this means for how the body is situated spatially, and indeed how understanding the body in its spatial environment is fundamental to understanding what self-tracking or body monitoring entail, and how they should be understood; and on how this has been entangled historically with technological design and innovation. As we will argue, this also has implications for the way that we can understand the relationship between the non-representational or sensory embodied experiences that self-tracking entails, and the representational forms that self-tracking data takes on in the present.

Data privacy historically

A technology that historically raised concerns about the privacy of personal bodily data was in the nineteenth century when the development of X-ray technology marked the first time it became possible to actually look below the surface of the body. Wilhelm Conrad Röntgen discovered what he first described as 'a new kind of rays' on 8 November 1895 (Segrè 1980: 21). At the time, physicists (Röntgen among them) were just beginning to experiment with cathode ray tubes. On 8 November, Röntgen had placed a Hittorf tube in a cardboard box, turned off the lights in the room and noticed how a special screen treated with barium platinum-cyanide began to glow when he activated his tube. When he placed objects between the tube and the screen, they appeared as shadow images of themselves. To his surprise, when he placed his hand between the tube and the screen, his flesh seemed to melt away, leaving a clear image of the bones in his hand. He was so shocked by the discovery that he was at first unsure that he could truly believe his eyes, and he spent seven weeks experimenting with the tube and screen to convince himself (22).

Röntgen published the results of this work in the first days of January 1896. Along with the paper, he included photographs of hands in which the skin and flesh had been rendered transparent but the bones of the hand and fingers were clearly visible. His results, and the images he had provided with his paper, immediately went viral (or as viral as was possible in the last years of the nineteenth century). Röntgen and his peers did not fully understand what types of rays were responsible for facilitating this new way of seeing the body, and thus the name 'X-ray' in which the 'X' stood for the unknown. However, the images he produced were a very concrete and manifest way of representing the current cutting edge of science and its potential (Simon 2004: 274). It was now apparent that the boundaries of sight and how one could look at the body and examine it had been stretched. The surface of the skin was no longer the limit; the secrets of the interior were now accessible to a rapidly expanding public.

Having heard about Röntgen's new discovery, and not wanting to be left behind, Thomas Edison rushed to his laboratory to attempt to duplicate Röntgen's results. He succeeded in doing this within weeks of the announcement of Röntgen's success, and by mid-March he had invented the 'fluoroscope', which he later developed into a hand-held model that people could use and experience at amusement parks, fairs and exhibitions. The fluoroscope didn't produce photographs, but it did allow people to hold up their hands to the instrument and instantly see through their skin to their bones. For many this was a thrilling new form of technology, and a completely novel way of seeing themselves, but for others the technology was disquieting. As Linda Simon has pointed out in her discussion of the consequences of the birth of this 'dark light':

> A view of one's skeleton 'within the enshrouding flesh' as one observer described it, looked too much like seeing one's bodily remains; these visions of the body's interior seemed analogous to an autopsy thrilling but ghoulish. (277)

With the advent of X-ray technology came a new era of seeing and thinking about the potential of what could be seen. The X-ray opened the interior of the body to the peering eye in a manner that some found to be ghoulish, but it simultaneously threw into question the issue of how the potential of this technology could be used and controlled. Rumours rapidly spread about the development of X-ray opera glasses, prompting politicians in the United States to introduce legislation banning the use of such spectacles (Swiderski 2012: 47). People contemplated what it might mean to be able to gaze through objects and companies developed lines of undergarments which they promised would protect the wearer from the peering potential of X-ray vision. Indeed, since its conception, X-ray vision has occupied an ambivalent position: lodged somewhere in the public conscience between a joke and a moral threat, where comic books of the 1950s and 1960s offered teenage boys the possibility of purchasing X-ray glasses for the low price of a dollar. Modern digital technology of the new millennium began to offer high-tech variations of the theme. Included here was everything from X-ray cameras to YouTube videos that demonstrate how the filters in Photoshop could be manipulated to allow users to seemingly dissolve layers of clothing.

In ways that resonate with current concerns about privacy and self-tracking technologies, there were fears that the new X-ray technology could destabilize and threaten the border between private and public domains, because if X-rays could penetrate to layers below the skin, it was feared that they might also be harnessed to provide people with a new and invasive form of vision. Indeed, it might be argued that it is precisely such an invasive form of vision that self-tracking data is enabling. We take up some of these issues in Chapter 5, where we discuss how people understand the data through which they can see their bodies, and Chapter 6, where we discuss the anticipatory modes through which people consider and sense the consequences of personal data.

Conclusion

In this chapter we have developed an historical perspective which offers us insights into how now ubiquitous technologies of knowing about the body have emerged through historical processes of research and design, and become part of ordinary everyday lives and institutionalized processes, through an examination of the history of the mirror, and to a lesser extent the weight scale.

Both technologies have participated in changes in how the body can be seen, sensed, learned about and known. They have also both become ubiquitous technologies that have endured into today's world in ways that are connected to the very technologies that are used for self-tracking. For example, smartphone cameras are used as mirrors and weight-scale data can be uploaded directly to platforms accessed through smartphone apps.

The technologies of glass, the convex lens and the mirror in particular opened up new possibilities for seeing and representing the body that the wealthy were able to adopt in ways that extended their existing modes of representing and contemplating themselves and others. Significantly, however, as our analysis of the history of Skokloster has shown, they did not only represent new ways of knowing about bodies but also they *situated* bodies spatially in ways that were meaningful in relation to their social, built and wider environments: as glass windows illuminated the indoor world in homes; as increasingly accurate paintings situated Wrangel in a particular material landscape and social position; and as mirrors enabled people to contemplate the social environment in which they and others participated from a new perspective. These technological innovations were also implicated in shifts in the modes of the visualization in society during these periods, and their relationality to the sensoriality of both everyday and medicalized experience of the human body. These representational and non-representational modes of experiencing the body and the emotions, as we show in the following chapters, can be traced through to contemporary ways of understanding the tracked body both through representational information and sensed experience.

4

Algorithmic Imaginations

Self-tracking devices and their software often promise, either explicitly or implicitly, to provide potential users with solutions to imagined everyday problems, such as coping with stressful situations, figuring out how to eat and workout properly, or how to sleep better. The discourse surrounding these technologies assumes 'that people need data streams and algorithms in order to reflect on, and engage in, self-discovery and self-exploration' (Ruckenstein and Pantzar 2017: 412). Answering to such a discourse, these technologies are algorithmic in the sense that they interpret and visualize data following protocols that, like algorithms in general, 'name both a problem and the steps by which it should be solved' (Gillespie 2014: 167). At the core of these promises lies an assumption of self-improvement that revolves around the belief that bodies, selves and lives can be improved and even optimized as long as people follow the mediated advice from their apps and devices, learn about themselves to gain an increased self-knowledge and change their habits and personal futures accordingly.

This chapter explores how self-tracking devices, and the digital infrastructures through which they are connected, 'think', how they perceive of the people that use and engage with them, and how they interpret their everyday lives and their imagined problems. Whereas in Chapter 1 we reviewed how similar discourses are shaped and argued for in the field of human–computer interaction (HCI) research, and offered an alternative approach, in this chapter we discuss how the design of self-tracking devices and their potential value for users are explained both by designers themselves and in various forms of promotional and instructional materials. Looking more closely at how technologies of this kind invite and encourage people to engage with them allows us to understand how they suggest possible futures for their users as well as what they expect and want from users in the present. Approaching the anticipated futures that are built into these technologies, while at the same time exploring the expectations and assumptions on which their design builds, is important for understanding how they provide a certain spatiality in and through which users are supposed to understand themselves and deal with the contingencies of everyday life.

We first turn to the Jawbone UP wristband in order to explore how this technology builds on a certain understanding of people and their everyday lives, and how it feels to follow the advice that it provides. Second, we look closely at two devices – the Narrative wearable camera clip and the Moodmetric 'smart' ring – which, rather than providing advice for personal enhancement, claim to help users to observe and understand what is going on in the present. Finally, we explore the Apple Health platform to see how it, as an example of a self-tracking system that is built into smartphones, claims to provide users with an understanding of the complexity of their health and activities, yet at the same time limits the possibilities for different devices and apps to connect with each other in a meaningful way. Exploring how these technologies and platforms are presented as potentially valuable for users, the chapter provides insights into the questions, hopes and dreams that become the very rationale for the design of self-tracking technologies and sheds light over the assumed problems that these technologies are supposed to solve through the recording, processing and visualization of data. Throughout the chapter we discuss how these technologies and imagined problems can be understood as sociocultural products underpinned by not only design imaginaries but also as deeply intertwined with the structural and temporal characteristics of contemporary society.

Anticipating the future self

As we described in the Prologue, the four of us used the Jawbone UP wristband on a daily basis during a period of time to record our activities and sleep patterns (see Pink, Fors and Berg 2017). On the company website, jawbone. com, the wristband was marketed with the words 'There's a better version of you out there, get UP and find it!' and we were all very excited and attracted by

– if not also sceptical of – the thought of wearing a device that could guide us through such a transformation. In the following we carve out an understanding of how this technology needs to conceptualize people and their everyday lives in order to make its advice meaningful.

The UP system is powered by the 'Smart Coach', an algorithmic technology that, unlike 'other canned fitness advisors out there', is 'like a partner in fitness – an intelligent guide that helps guide you to healthier choices each and every day'. Instead of simply using self-tracking data as a point of reference for personal reflection, the UP system claims to provide meaning to the numbers through big data analysis and machine learning processes that compare user data with data of other similar users in their global user database. The system, it is said, 'will come to learn all your habits – both the good and the bad – like that healthy friend or personal trainer who is always motivating you and cheering you on'. Putting great trust into the possibilities of machine learning, the people behind this technology appear to assume that there is something of a hidden code in people that can (and needs to) be cracked. With the proper amount and kind of data, the wristband is imagined to develop an understanding of users that unfolds over time and that is used as a basis for providing coaching and advice that 'go deeper and get more personalized' by crunching personal data 'into actionable insights and uniquely personalized guidance'. It seems to be assumed that the Jawbone UP wristband has the potential to know users better than they – relying on their sensory embodied experiences and gut-feelings – could possibly know themselves. This perspective was advanced further by Kelvin Kwong (2015), who was senior product manager and head of behaviour change at Jawbone. Kwong explains the presumed benefits of the UP self-tracking wristband:

> 'It's getting late! Don't you think you should get to bed?' my father asked, poking his head into my bedroom. When I was 15 years old, this happened a couple times each week. A decade and a half later, and what's changed? Not much actually. My tendency to stay up late continues, but what's different is the nudge. Instead of my father intervening, my nudges now come from an intelligent system called Smart Coach.

Although the Jawbone device is quite similar to other self-tracking technologies, it stands out by underscoring the importance of big data analytics since it 'crunches your data into actionable insights and uniquely personalized guidance' and aims at providing something more than an 'activity dashboard'. Instead, this personalized system wants to guide users 'every step of the way to a better, healthier you' by turning 'raw data into your personal fitness advisor'. Kwong (2015) continues to explain how the Smart Coach works by getting to 'know' the users and their routines:

> My Smart Coach knows that I typically wake up around 7:00 am, so if I'm still awake at 12:30 am, it can tell that something is awry. But unlike my father, Smart Coach crunches my data 24/7 (no offense, dad) and points out that for every 30 minutes I'm up past my normal bedtime, I tend to be 8% less active the next day.

By following the suggestions provided by the system, users are assumed to find themselves making better everyday choices, by going beyond 'knowing' what is good for us, to actually 'doing' it. Kwong (2015) underscores that 'closing the gap between "should" and "will" is where the human mind gets hung up', and therefore it is critical to receive a suggestion from the app 'with the right context, delivered in just the right way' on what to do and when and how it should be done. The idea is that the app should learn about the users – 'tune in' to them and their daily lifestyles – in order to create an awareness of how their lifestyle habits affect their overall health, sleep and movement patterns, and on the basis of this, guide users towards healthier decisions. Not only is this device believed to be able to learn about individual users and their habits but also to identify and decipher unique correlations between habits and activities. The 'active coaching', as the service is labelled, builds on 'behavioral science techniques' and is supposed to improve the overall well-being of users and create an experience that helps them achieve their health aspirations. For instance, they conclude that the system helps 'people get to bed 23 minutes earlier on average and move 27% more during the day'. Aiming to guide and motivate users with respect to their particular situation, routines and abilities, the Smart Coach is supposed to deliver a message with the right context, in just the right way. When we used the wristband and app in our auto-ethnographic experiment, we did indeed receive feedback and suggestions based on our activities. Martin, for instance, was advised to walk at least 13,671 steps per day during the following week, and this led him to jot down the following field notes:

This number might seem random but it was an average of the last two days' activities and during the weekend I had taken quite a long walk. Although it did seem difficult to take that amount of steps while at the same time having a week full of meetings, commuting and writing, I accepted the challenge. I did, however, fail. It took quite a while until I was given more recommendations. It was as if the app was disappointed in me; as if it thought of me as a quitter, as if it didn't want to play with me anymore. I started wondering what the app was thinking and indeed *if* it was thinking. When should it get in touch with me again and give ideas, challenges and recommendations?

The recommendations lacked context and came with a frequency and style that was unexpected, yet very precise. This made Martin nearly obsessed with providing the app with data, by running frequently and making detours of various lengths just to keep those steps counting, simply as a way to respond. The app demanded us to engage in activities with an exact output and it did not understand the context of our everyday lives, nor could it explain how it was thinking, or 'tune in' to our lives and offer an opening for negotiation. In the field notes, Martin recorded this frustrating experience:

> I was tired, had just taken a shower and started walking on and off, almost naked, in my flat just to reach the 10,000 steps. I directly crashed in bed afterwards. It felt bizarre and I was happy that no one could see me doing this silly thing. It made [me] think though, what the difference was between 9,700 steps and the 10,000. Would those extra 300 steps actually make a difference? The simple language of steps was both attractive and irritating. It felt as if we, the app and I, were lost in translation when our mission was to find my better self.

The difficulty in understanding the contextual advice that the device promised to provide made us wonder what was actually going on under the hood of this device. It sometimes felt as if the app made a fool out of us, either by asking if the regular walk to the coffee shop should be registered as a workout or, similar to how Kwong imagined the wristband in the quote at the beginning of this section, by acting as a dominant parent giving orders without any reasonable explanation. One evening the app asked Martin to go to bed at 9.57 pm the following night since that would be a good way to prepare for 'a brainy day'. It could (or would) not provide any reason for choosing this particular time, and neither did it provide any kind of context or explanation. The day after the following lines were written in his field notes:

> Here I am at 8 pm. I haven't had dinner and I definitely don't want to go running. But there are 5,000 steps to go until I reach my goal. I just came home from work and somehow I have to fix the situation. I feel stressed out. And the app tells me that I have to go to bed at 9.57. I want to have a glass of wine, have something [to] eat and think about stuff. Oh well, I guess I just wanted to say something about my dissatisfaction right now.

By giving arbitrary and indeed also contradictory advice on different activities, in this case movement and sleep, the app seemed to know something about us that it neither could nor would share. At the same time, it felt as if we, as users on our quest to find our better selves, were simply thought of as machines or mechanisms without souls, desires and any form of social context outside of the app. It was almost as if the app demanded us to please it by providing data, by following advice and by trying to figure out what might be a good thing to do, what the meaning of our activity could possible be and what the app might do with the data. There is an obvious tension between life as *experienced* by users and as *imagined* by designers, and as we have seen in the above it is assumed that people lack a fundamental reflexive self-understanding, and it is imagined that taking control over one's life in the pursuit for a better self requires access to data-driven advice. At the same time this system imagines and perhaps also requires users to live in a world that is foreseeable, with a structured temporality and where the everyday is not shaped by contingencies but instead by a presupposed procedurality that resembles the computational logic of algorithms on which devices such as the UP wristband rely (see Beer 2016; Dourish 2016).

Augmenting the present

The example of our experience of Jawbone helped us learn how self-tracking technologies and their algorithmic interpretations of personal data are assumed to help users establish an understanding of themselves over time. We now approach two somewhat different technologies, the Narrative Clip (Fors, Berg and Pink 2016) and the Moodmetric ring (Berg 2017), that take a different approach to supporting users. Instead of collecting data over time, comparing them with those of other users and providing algorithmic advice, these technologies claim to help users understand their bodies and everyday lives in the present by tuning into particular situations and moments, and using them as point of reference to learn about life as it is lived. These two devices both claim to allow for an augmentation of the present through which people not only can learn about themselves but also encounter new dimensions of their lives when being reviewed using the devices' companion apps. As we show below, these technologies build on similar assumptions concerning how people live their lives, yet their technological offerings are framed in a somewhat different way, which helps us to further nuance the idea of the human body as 'a data-generating device that must be coupled to sensor technology and analytic algorithms in order to be known' (Schüll 2016: 326; see also Viseu and Suchman 2010; Hansen 2014).

As we discussed above, self-tracking devices are often imagined to help users to make healthier choices and to gain control over their bodies and habits. Other devices of this kind, such as the Narrative Clip (Narrative n.d.), offer users memory assistance and the possibility to 're-live' moments of their lives, so that moments that would otherwise pass them by would not be forgotten. This device is said to be the world's smallest wearable automatic camera that provides users with a 'searchable and shareable photographic memory' (Kickstarter 2012). In a promotional video, a speaker voice presents the gadget as a tiny wearable camera that automatically captures two geotagged photos of the surroundings every minute and organizes these photos in an app library. Such a device is assumed to come in handy since:

> Life rushes by, and you just try to keep up. But too often you can't recall what you did last summer. Or last weekend. Or even last morning. We try to capture the moment we think are special, or important, like birthdays, weddings, holidays, things like that. But the most important moments are the ones we didn't realize were moments until afterwards. (Kickstarter 2012)

The Narrative Clip is said to help users find the meaningful moments in life and make it possible to 'relive' certain parts of one's life as it is remembered. 'Sometimes the best moments in life are the simple ones, the things that pass us by without even noticing' the company explains in another promotional video. They wanted this 'ultimate lifelogging device' to capture the 'small surprises, and the everyday experiences' and avoid letting these moments become forgotten (Kickstarter 2012). Through interviews with the people behind the Narrative Clip we approached how they imagined automatic digital photographing, and it became clear that this wearable device was imagined to capture an 'authentic' picture of the world in which the user is situated. One of the interviewees stated that the camera clip would allow users to capture 'the honesty in your life' and to register 'people's true facial expressions'. There is a strong sense of an assumed authenticity in the way that the designers frame the camera; as if there would actually be a recordable world out there and as if that actually would add to the authentic picture of everyday life. Or perhaps that the camera allows us to gain access to what is perceived of as authentic. The human actor as a spectator in everyday life is assumed to give up the embodied and emplaced gaze by which they interpret what is going on in the particular context that affects the way technologies and the produced visual material are both imagined and treated. Therefore, an idea of everyday life emerges in which the fleeting 'magical' moments of our lives are recordable, re-liveable, re-presented and remembered through the use of these technologies.

However, there is a tension between how the body is rendered by the designers as both the primary source for experiencing and embracing the moment and as an obstacle that gets in the way for cognitive meaning-making of past experiences in everyday life. Thus, only an automatic camera can produce evidence or invocations for what actually happened that can be remembered through a cognitive process of structuring memories around the produced photographs. The tension becomes evident as an ontological question if the environment is something that is there to objectively be observed and looked at or as one to be embodied and lived in, while simultaneously the Narrative Clip is conceptualized as a reflective device that provides opportunities to rethink what happened without disrupting the embodied sensation of being there. These different perspectives on the relationship between the body, mind and environment create particular possible routes to develop this visual life-logging device further, while simultaneously closing off other routes, and we discuss this particular example further in Chapter 6.

The idea that a device allows for a level of authenticity and 'honesty' that goes beyond the experiential limits of the human body is present in the descriptions of the Moodmetric device, which is said to be a 'smart' ring that is accompanied by an app claiming to help 'people to learn about their mind and emotions' (Moodmetric 2017). The Moodmetric developer's website asserts that using the ring allows people to understand how 'different circumstances affect you' emotionally (Moodmetric 2017). Wearing the device is assumed to assist users in knowing when they experience stress, and to help them identify the moments that make them calm. Referring to herself and her own experiences during a panel discussion on 'The Future of Wearables for Health & Wellness' at a Biohacker Summit held in Finland, Niina Venho, CEO of the company that makes Moodmetric, suggested that the device allows users to engage in a process of learning where the data produced by the device are used to interpret what is going on in the body (Biohacker Summit 2015). Her argument was that the majority of people have difficulty in recognizing their feelings using their embodied perceptions alone and therefore need a device like Moodmetric:

> You think you feel something but it's something else actually. But most people understand: yes, I'm really stressed now, but most people don't know what to do about it. That's why people go on long … uhm … leaves, because they can't handle it all at work.

During the panel discussion, Venho elaborated on her explanation of the device and said that learning about oneself was actually at the core of their idea for the product:

> We are not always expecting everyone to wear this day and night [for the] whole [of] their lives. Maybe people learn something. You might be wearing the Moodmetric ring for three months and know everything about yourself and find out the best methods to wind down or whatever. And maybe you just abandon the ring and … eh … I wouldn't be upset about that, if you learned something. I really wish that people would know something more.

The Moodmetric is designed to help users 'find out something about their minds', as Venho puts it during the above-mentioned panel discussion. The emphasis on learning not only assumes that users do not know about themselves sufficiently but also points towards a move away from an assumed accuracy in the data produced by the devices, to an emphasis on how the data can become part of embodied practices and experiences. In Venho's account, the Moodmetric answers to quite a specific dimension of the human body to which we are assumed to have little access. Humans 'are made of carbon, water and emotions', as she stated in the discussion, and using the ring as part of everyday life activities it becomes possible to become more self-aware of one's feelings. This is achieved by learning about 'what makes you react, what makes you feel intensely … [and] what makes you calm your mind' (Venho 2015a). In one of the many blog posts on their company's website, where Venho and colleagues explore the different affordances of the Moodmetric, she shares some experiences from using the ring during a game of 'Texas Hold'em', a card game. Having used the ring during the whole game, she used the visualization of her emotions generated by the ring to manually recall and explore different phases of the game and how good and bad hands of cards affected her mind and emotions (Venho 2015b). The Moodmetric app provides the user with a circular diagram with a radius that changes according to the users' mood level. In the blog post, Venho used this visualization as a map where certain phases of the game were jotted down. Her notes suggest that her mood level spikes when losing or winning a big hand, and that she is fairly calm when waiting or simply bored. In addition to these notes, a series of photographs depicting her hand of cards or the chips that she managed to win are shared in the blog post. These photos are marked with her current mood level and it appears that she uses the data as a means to understand how well she is keeping her poker face. As this example tells us, the data produced by the Moodmetric is assumed to provide insights about what the user is imagined to *actually* feel and experience in a certain situation. As Venho (2015b) explains, the data produced by the device is believed to give access to what such a games night looks 'like in the eyes of the autonomic nervous system'. The poker face metaphor is valuable in this context since it allows us to grasp the tension between the body as known through experience and as known through data. The body is imagined to produce infallible data, yet at the same time it is understood as hopelessly incapable of making sense of the data it produces without technological assistance.

Dealing with complexity

Apple Health is a pre-installed app that works as a digital health hub on iPhones around the world. It is presented in a colourful and inviting way, and offers users a 'bold way to look at your health' (Apple 2019) through its centralized health data processing, analysis and visualization. The app is described as a mechanism that makes the practice of self-tracking more convenient and powerful, and it is designed to help users with understanding their bodies and everyday lives so that that they can make any necessary lifestyle changes in the pursuit of better overall health. Apple Health is designed to make 'it easy to learn about your health and start reaching your goals' since it consolidates data from different apps and devices, including the iPhone's built in motion sensors, and provides users with a data overview where they can learn about their 'progress in one convenient place' (Apple 2019). The app builds on the idea that any understanding of health requires several data sources to fully engage with the complexity of the human body. Apple has grouped the various data sources that can be processed by the app and explains that there are 'Four keys to a healthy life. Right at your fingertips,' namely activity, sleep, mindfulness and nutrition. These dimensions are said to play 'an important role in your overall health — and in the app', thereby framing the app as a dashboard to the human body where users can look at their stats throughout the day in order to 'stay on track'. The Health app is further presented through a series of short video clips, where a calm voice explains how using the app can lead to serious changes in life, not the least since, as Apple put it, 'once you start using the Health app, there's no stopping you'. In one of the video clips a general introduction to the app is provided:

> Staying healthy. It can feel complicated. Truth is, making small changes in four key areas can make a difference. Just move a little more, eat a little better, sleep tighter, and take a moment to calm your mind. Everything's connected. When you move more, you tend to feel less stressed. If you sleep better, you tend to eat better. One good change leads to another, and another. Pretty soon, healthy decisions start feeling better than unhealthy ones. Check in, see how you're doing, and track your progress over time. When you know your health better, you know yourself better. Simple really. (Apple 2019)

The Apple Health system is supposed to inspire users to move a little bit more, to sleep a little longer, to eat better and to engage a little more often in mindfulness exercises. Given their visual style, the short video clips are clearly aimed at people with tight schedules, heaps of deadlines and generally 'busy lives' where 'our minds can get pretty restless'. In these presentations it is suggested that there is a need for people to hand over the control of their lives to the Health app, which will assist them to 'understand what habits we need to break', to find 'a natural rhythm', to engage in activities that get 'your heart pumping' and to otherwise handle the fact that 'our brains aren't wired to be constantly switched on'. Each of the video clips ends with an animated illustration of a heart that smoothly transforms into the Apple logo. The symbolic language of the video clips is clear: Apple wants us to know that they want to, and indeed can, take care of people. Apple Health is described as 'helping' users to manage and visualize certain dimensions of their lives, in order to 'keep all your health and fitness information under your control and in one place on your device'. This means the Health app entails more than simply a hub or a nexus for interconnected health and fitness apps. Rather, it is imagined as a tool that allows for a more comprehensive understanding of the users, and their bodies and minds. The idea that people are enabled to know themselves better is key for Apple Health. Moreover, by presenting an allegedly inclusive and holistic, yet in reality predefined and limited, collection of data types, the app gives the impression that it can grasp the complexity of users' bodies and lives.

Apple Health and similar systems such as Google Fit are becoming increasingly important parts of the digital health ecosystem, since they allow devices and apps to interconnect and share databases, algorithms and data streams. Broker platforms of this kind, as Van Dijck and Poell (2016) label them, organize and direct data streams and interactions between users and devices, and set up the boundaries for how the devices can engage in processes of datafication through which various aspects of a user's physical or mental well-being is quantified and translated into data. As Van Dijck and Poell (2016) argue, it is increasingly difficult for these technologies to operate independently without being entangled with other apps, devices and databases in the ecosystem. This potential to combine and distribute different kinds of data in ways makes 'individual platforms prisoners of the larger connective ecosystem' (Van Dijck and Poell 2016: 8; see also Van Dijck, Poell and de Waal 2018). Put differently, despite the promises of apps such as Apple Health to allow users to understand the complexity of their personal health, broker platforms tend to standardize and limit the possible data types that can be used for such measurements. Not only do they dictate which data types are perceived of as important for understanding personal health, but they also indicate how and through what measurements such data types should be understood. Instead of adapting to users and their unique lifestyles to provide personalized advice, as self-tracking technologies often claim to do, they require users to follow the ideal and standardized paths through the everyday. As Ruckenstein (2014: 69) argues, these devices make formerly 'unknown' aspects of bodies and lives more 'detectable', 'transparent' and 'visible', yet it must be noted that these aspects and the metrics used to measure them are always decided beforehand since algorithms and databases can only digest and fit certain forms of data that, like all other technologies, result from certain social and cultural contexts. This means that broker platforms such as Apple Health create boundaries from a predefined list of data types which provide users with a kind of digital spatiality in which they are invited to understand themselves and their lives. Users are thus invited to participate in a conditioned and directed learning process where they are assumed to engage with their data and take notice of how certain kinds of data correlate with others, yet without inventing new data types or in other ways finding new and creative ways of measuring themselves. This implies that the contingencies and embodied experiences that normally guide people through the everyday are avoided since these dimensions of people's lives simply are not 'algorithm ready' (Gillespie 2014), that is, they are not ready to be packaged and scaled in ways that make them fit into databases and parse through APIs (application programming interfaces), to be compared with data from other people and apps where they will become objects of algorithmic procedures. The backstage parts of self-tracking devices and apps and the limitations of their technological design are rarely presented to users. The user-oriented app Apple Health, for instance, is structured by the Apple HealthKit API on a technical level to which mainly designers and developers would turn. In the technical documentation of Apple HealthKit, the API is described as a means to add value to the general user experience of a health and fitness app:

> Integrate HealthKit into your health and fitness apps for iOS and watchOS to create a more seamless user experience. When a customer provides permission for your app to read and write health and activity data to their

Health app, your app becomes a valuable data source and can deliver deeply informed health and fitness solutions. (Apple Developer 2019)

The HealthKit is a framework that was introduced with iOS 8, and it allows apps to save and access health and fitness-related data such as weight, step count, nutritional information, blood pressure, glucose levels and some sixty other data types. When Apple HealthKit is presented at developers' conferences or in developer-oriented readings, it is commonly described with an emphasis on what the data can do and what can be done to the data rather than what kind of data are allowed to be included. The combination of different data sources as such, rather than the kinds of data that are actually involved, are sometimes thought of as having nearly magic qualities. In a HealthKit-oriented session at Apple's Worldwide Developers Conference 2014, engineer Terry Worley explained that this API is 'uniquely positioned to be the key component to finally bring together all of these accessories, all of these health and fitness apps, by consolidating the data into one centralised source'. This would, as he imagined, lead to a wide spectrum of 'opportunities', some of which he explained by sharing a personal experience:

> In fact, HealthKit is so powerful that it can transform a software engineer, like me, just by working on it. Someone who shuns the daylight, who spends years sitting behind the computer, living my life by the light of my displays. Some of you can probably relate to that. Now, working on HealthKit, I'm using a standing workstation. I am riding my bike to work, and I'm even wearing a heart rate chest strap on my bike rides. (ASCIIwwdc 2014)

According to Apple, the HealthKit framework 'is designed to share data between apps in a meaningful way'. Although there is room to make a certain app focus on certain metrics, app developers cannot create custom data types or units but can only choose from the predefined list of data types and units provided by Apple, to ensure that any connected apps 'understand' what a certain data type means and the ways in which it can be used. There are five categories for body measurements; the HealthKit relies on certain measurements and constants that can used to communicate with other apps. In addition, these data points are connected to a number of subclasses and parameters that together produce hierarchies and relationships between different units and data points. What HealthKit does is not only to dictate what sort of data types are possible but also to structure certain relationships between different kinds of data. Some kinds of data are fixed and some are more fluid. But, importantly, what counts as health data is determined in advance, and in that way the body and the self that we are supposed to know better through the use of these apps are also delimited.

Conclusion

Marketers and designers of self-tracking devices, apps and systems present their offerings to potential users by explaining how such technologies can help them to learn about their bodies and everyday lives, and how to adjust their lifestyle to lead a life that is healthier, more productive and perhaps also more mindful. This chapter has engaged with a series of examples through which we have learned that self-tracking technologies involve an anticipation of the user's future self, an imagined possibility to augment the present and thereby support users in understanding the environment in which they are situated as well as supporting users in dealing with the complexity involved in self-tracking using several data sources. Although these examples highlight different aspects of what self-tracking technologies are believed to do and how they are imagined to become part of people's lives, they share the assumption that people not only can improve themselves but indeed also that they to some extent need such an improvement. In these accounts, people are often imagined, however implicitly, as slightly dysfunctional and in need of guidance and repair since they and their bodies, as Schüll (2016) puts it, are believed to be 'constitutionally ill equipped to make rational, healthy choices'. The ways in which self-tracking technologies imagine their potential users is paradoxical since they are simultaneously positioned on the one hand as passive and complex, mysterious and difficult to decode, and on the other as active as well as machine-like and nearly algorithmically structured; as subjects that might take control of their lives if they get the proper guidance, a nudge in the right time and place, along with proper and timely interpretations of what is going on in and around their bodies. In these examples, the very access to data and data-driven advice is often imagined to help users to learn about themselves in ways that simply would not be possible using experience and reflection alone. This means that self-tracking technologies of this kind build on an understanding of users as desiring an alternative future and claim to offer routes to such a future as long as their advice and/or data are followed and correctly interpreted. Such routes often involve a somewhat paradoxical solution where social problems are imagined as solvable by using algorithms and cognitive psychology. For instance, seeing the apps as a remedy for a sense of losing control in a messy, complex and stressful urban life is frequently used when self-tracking devices are presented and their value discussed by designers and marketers at conventions and product pitches. Such scenarios are projected through a nearly behaviouristic lens where users and their bodies are imagined as both docile and not only eager to be mastered but also to be ready to live a life that follows the algorithmic logic of these technologies and their anticipated temporalities of well-being (Berg 2017). Such technologies thus allow only for certain programmed futures by deciding in advance what counts as usable data, how these data should be interpreted and visualized and how people should engage with these data. Despite the claimed personalization and adaptability of these systems, it must be noted that they are designed with algorithms and assumptions of certain physiological and psychological models at their core, with the intention of 'augmenting, mediating and governing the ways in which individuals and social groups engage with their own bodies and health, and transforming the ways that people undertake physical activity' (Williamson 2015: 134). Furthermore, self-tracking devices are often connected to infrastructures such as Apple Health in order to connect and share data with other apps, with the intention to allow for a more complex data analysis to take place. This implies that the capabilities of a certain device or app not only are guided by the interpretative repertoire of its designers but also of the limitations that are built into a broker platform, such as Apple Health, that invites users not only to engage in certain forms of self-tracking but also to certain forms of learning and self-knowledge.

5

Traces through the Present

In this chapter we explore how people engage with and often exceed the imagined worlds of the designers of self-tracking technologies. Through our ethnographies of everyday self-tracking we outline the modes of engagement and resistance through which the demands of the apps discussed in Chapter 4 are received, and explore the implications of this in determining if people's commitments to self-tracking and personal data endure.

To undertake this we put the question of how people learn and know through self-tracking and personal data at the centre of our analysis. In doing so we account for the sensory ways of knowing this entails. We examine how people improvise ways of using self-tracking technologies that expand on or go beyond the categories of activity the technologies are designed to measure, and deviate from how personal data is imagined to be activated by the developers. We ask what this enables people to imagine and feel instead. Approaching this question through the concept of learning enables us to scrutinize the disjunctures between intended and actual use. This involves examining how the potential of personal data is imagined by developers and how these imaginaries are informed by their understandings of processes of knowledge production and self-improvement through self-tracking. We compare the pedagogies represented by the idea that personal data can be part of such a self-improvement agenda with ethnographic examples of how personal data actually becomes activated and imbued with meaning in people's everyday lives. By 'the present' we refer to the moments in which life is lived and known and where self-tracking and personal data become meaningful rather than to the controversial notion of the continuous 'ethnographic present'. This forms the basis upon which we propose that the future of personal data needs to be rethought in Chapter 6, in which we turn to the anticipatory modes of thinking about and experiencing self-tracking and personal data in the everyday worlds of users and technology designers.

This chapter is based in ethnographic research focusing on aspects of self-tracking that are embedded in how people experience their everyday environments but that are often not normally spoken about or represented in public contexts. We discuss the experiences of participants who we refer to as *everyday self-trackers*, with whom we have undertaken ethnographic research in Australia and Sweden between 2014 and 2017. The participants in this group used their self-tracking devices routinely in personal habits and ways of doing things: for example, their movements, sleep, food intake and sometimes heart rate. They consisted of broadly middle-class people living in the cities of Melbourne, Australia, and Halmstad and Stockholm, Sweden, working in mainly professional roles and in education, the public sector, the arts and IT. With these participants we used a combination of sensory ethnography interview and GoPro methods that enabled us to engage empathetic ways of knowing (about and with) the experiences participants discussed and a sense of attunement to their experiences as they recounted their uses of the technologies, and showed us the tactile and visual ways in which they engaged with apps and data. Through these methods, we were able to identify the unspoken and tacit aspects of the participants' self-tracking activities that concerned how their personal data production activities became imbued with meaning: how the data felt and were experienced as part of wider social, spatial and physical environments.

In Chapter 1 we introduced our critique of assumptions that self-tracking and personal data have been considered to lead to behaviour change. We first elaborate on this by discussing how the epistemological status of personal data is construed in technology-focused research and development, and the implications for this for how learning processes are understood and described. We will then develop an alternative route to conceptualizing learning in relation to anthropological perspectives on how knowledge develops through people's social and sensory experiences of being part of different practices in different environments. This theoretical background corresponds with what we have learned about people's experiences of self-tracking. We end by suggesting rethinking what people can learn with personal data and self-tracking technologies, and in doing so demonstrate how the pedagogical design anthropology approach to how we learn with technologies introduced in Chapter 1 can be mobilized.

Technical imaginaries of data-driven learning

Alongside recent developments in digital self-tracking devices and apps, a growing field of research in information systems and interaction design has focused on technology that facilitates the collection and use of personally relevant information: personal informatics (PI). The ideas that underpin PI are of interest here due to how they are intertwined with the technical development of the actual self-tracking devices and thereby condition how they work, how they are designed and how their intended use is demonstrated by developers and designers (see Chapter 4). Kersten-van Dijk and colleagues' (2017) review of the field of PI refers to 'self-improvement hypothesis', which represents how it is imagined that people learn from their devices and apps, that is, 'Users obtain (self-)insights by examining their data and subsequently change their behavior based on these insights' (3). This is said to 'represent the dominant way of thinking about PI and the prevailing intention in designing such systems' (270). Across different studies within PI the process of obtaining 'self-insights' by examining the graphs and data points provided by the self-tracking apps is described as a part of people's goal-oriented agenda to change behaviours for particular reasons such as losing weight, becoming healthier or more fit, etc. Two particularly well-cited models of how this happens stand out: the 'five-stage model of personal informatics' (Li, Dey and Forlizzi 2010; 2011); and the 'lived informatics model of personal informatics' (Epstein et al. 2015). The former model emphasizes an iterative process of people's transition between preparation, collection, integration, reflection and action with an end goal of knowledge supporting behaviour change. The self-tracking devices in this case are imagined as objective technologies for optimizing and experimenting with the body, collecting neutral data, making them transparent and then reflecting/learning from it. The latter model proposes a broader understanding of how self-tracking manifests in the habits of the users. In this latter case, Epstein and colleagues (2015) point out that self-trackers do not only switch tools or quit self-tracking because the device does not fit their information needs (as proposed by Li, Dey and Forlizzi 2010), they switch tools for a variety of reasons based on everyday situations such as the device breaking, people changing phones or receiving a new recommendation (Rooksby et al. 2014). Through the 'lived informatics model', Epstein and colleagues suggest how the 'five-stage-model' can be expanded to better capture how people's different motivations make them use tools differently. Nevertheless, since the latter model is based on the former, both still rely on the self-improvement hypothesis. Both models draw on the idea that learning from tracking and personal data happens through an iterative process, where cognitive reflection fuels how people use the information given by the self-tracker, and the technology is assumed to underpin and rationalize human action.

However, Kersten-van Dijk and colleagues' (2017) review shows that there is in fact no direct evidence that the learning model that is implicitly active through the design of these apps and devices fully responds to how people use them. They conclude that more research is needed concerning how, why and when the learning model works. We expand this suggestion and argue that the disjunctures that emerge between the design world of body-monitoring apps and people's experiences of meaninglessness when trying to use them has to be understood by critically reviewing the deployed ideas of learning. By contesting the assumptions of the cognitive, linear and data-driven – that is, induced by data – learning theory that flows through the 'self-improvement hypothesis' (Kersten-van Dijk et al. 2017: 3) in HCI-research, we can deepen our understanding of why and how people engage with the body-monitoring apps in their present form and function (Fors and Pink 2017). We question if the interactional model of feedback interventions that 'serve to interrupt the flow of automatic, habitual decision-making, making room for a more controlled and rational decision-making process resulting in better (healthier, more productive) decisions and behaviors' (Kersten-van Dijk et al. 2017: 5) reflects what people are seeking when engaging these devices in their everyday lives. Even though self-tracking is intertwined with the body, the technical version of how to learn with the bodily data is remarkably disembodied. For example, one of our research participants, Jens, a computer scientist who specializes in sensors and apps that track physical movement, at one point during the interview started to sketch on a whiteboard how he imagined self-tracking devices interacted with the body. Figure 5.1 shows his drawing; to the left the human being is sketched as a brain and an arm, and there is a feedback loop that connects the device on the arm with the app that in turn interact with the brain. Jens' main concern was how to create an app that could learn from the personal data and give proper advice to the user on what to do to manage to change behaviour.

People variously engage or resist this agenda (Fors and Pink 2017). For instance, one Swedish participant, Ann-Christine, found the tracking device useless and tiresome, because, as she told Vaike, the fact that the app gave her information and push notices about how many steps she took did not make any difference to her. Since the app only showed her what she already knew, that she took very few steps every day, it did not motivate her to do anything differently. In fact, Ann-Christine described to us how instead she resisted the intended agenda since it did not feel meaningful to her:

> But it is not like, 'oh my God, I walk this little, now I must start to train'.
> It doesn't motivate me at all – I think that is really interesting, because I
> thought it would motivate me, or that I would get more … I already knew
> that I didn't move enough – When I saw it [in the app] I said to myself that
> I need to do something about this, and I asked myself what to do about it,
> well I don't know and then it didn't take me further – and the push notices
> [that you get from the app that gives you suggestions of what to do] they are

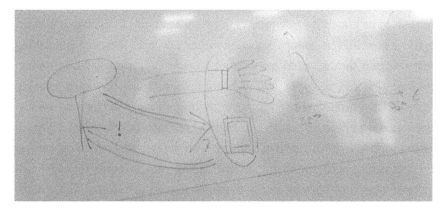

Figure 5.1 How learning through a self-tracking app is visualized by a computer scientist. Photo: Vaike Fors.

just like [putting the phone down on the table with a shrug of the shoulder] for me. They don't tell me anything. Some people are like that they will put in training sessions into their calendar and then they do it. My calendar has no impact on me whatsoever.

As this example indicates, the individual, cognitive-psychological and computer-centred perspectives on human and machine relationships outlined above are often not played out in everyday life experience. In the next section we demonstrate an alternative understanding of learning that highlights embodied and emplaced perspectives on knowing, and enables us to interpret how people integrate self-tracking devices and personal data into their everyday activities and imaginaries.

Sensory emplaced learning

The cognitive-psychological and computer-centred perspectives on human learning that have prevailed in research and development of self-tracking technologies have long since been contested along with calls to 'explore alternatives to studying people as objects to be modeled' (Whiteside and Wixon 1987: 355). Simultaneously, pragmatist and sociocultural theory have been part of an influential strand of learning theory focused on how human action and knowing is shaped by the use of cultural tools (such as technological artefacts) construed in the specific sociocultural contexts in which these actions take place (Wertch 1998; Lave and Wenger 1991), and how knowledge always develops in relation to its practical consequences in people's pursuits to manage life-based tasks. Knowledge is always knowing-in-practice and therefore something that you gain through participation, not a neutral and detached information package that can be gained through acquisition. These life-based learning theories have been developed in stark contrast to more didactic theories of institutional knowledge transfer. Such theories have developed in a critical relationship to cognitive ideas of learning, with the ambition of moving beyond the individual perspective and instead calling our attention to social and cultural aspects of learning and how the intellectual or material tools people use must be accounted for to understand the situatedness of learning. As a result, learning theory concerning human–technology relations has moved the research subagenda from solely investigating how people acquire knowledge through mental processing, to understanding that knowing is always attached to a knower in a specific environment and mediated by cultural tools. In the same vein, the question of what these tools mean to people has been nudged from being predominantly a question for the designer of the tool to decide, to instead become negotiated in the actual use of the tool. Meaning-making is therefore re-situated from a question of how well the learner has understood the intended meaning, to an open question of what meanings are given to the tools through their use in specific historic, social and material environments. One example of self-tracking researchers who take this stance are media scholars Stine Lomborg and Kirsten Frandsen (2016) who argue for the benefits of viewing self-tracking as acts of communication and thereby that 'meaning-making' is a key aspect of the appropriation and use of self-tracking technologies. In their interpretation, meaning-making of self-tracking is both informed by cognitive and affective capacities of the user and the context. In this scenario, the self-tracking tools are conceptualized as primarily communicative affordances.

However, even though sociocultural learning theories call for systematic attention to both the situatedness and experiential elements of learning, questions of cognition, language and conscious thought remain central (Hodkinson, Biesta and James 2008), With some exceptions (Berdugo and Nicely 2019; Lupton 2017; Pantzar and Ruckenstein 2017), theories of how learning is part of how we corporeally and sensorially experience the world, which highlight tacit and unspoken aspects of learning and knowing (Merleau-Ponty 1962; Ingold 2000), are often neglected in research on self-tracking. The use of media technologies in everyday life offers many opportunities to develop embodied forms of knowledge (Crossley 2001; Moores 2012) and participate in the mundane ways people make sense of the world, far beyond their role as providers of content and for communication. These routes to knowing might be difficult to articulate since people's life-world-based learning resources cannot be treated solely as content; they consist of knowing what is 'more-than-representational' (Lorimer 2005). The more-than-representational aspects of knowledge go beyond language and discourse. They involve sensory and emotional responses that sometimes cannot be easily articulated. For example, studies have shown how extensive use of digital photographing and photo-sharing apps orient users' attention specifically towards tacit and embodied experiences of daily life and how they can be shared with others. This everyday 'education of attention' (Gibson 1979: 254) has pedagogical implications for how people make sense of educational resources that are provided in other more-or-less pedagogically oriented settings (Fors 2013; 2015).

This approach to learning as processual, situated and embodied helped us to develop an approach through which we were able to learn with the participants about what anthropologists of knowledge have suggested is a way of knowing that comes about incrementally as they move through the world (for example, Ingold 2000; Pink 2015). This suggested that we might understand the ways of knowing that emerge from these participants' experiences of self-tracking as cumulative and ongoing rather than something that might be packaged and objectified as a unit of self-contained 'knowledge'. Instead, such ways of knowing are a form of everyday ongoing learning that may happen in ways that are not necessarily noticeable but are incremental and always unfinished. These ways of knowing are simultaneously ways of sensing the world and of making sense of data. Indeed, if we regard data as part of the world rather than something separate from it, knowing and sensing the environments we inhabit and move through and knowing and sensing data become inseparable within the same process. As we have argued elsewhere (Pink and Fors 2017) self-tracking is a perfect example that reinforces our argument that analytically we need to go beyond the models that emphasize sociotechnical relationships that have tended to dominate in sociological and geographical studies of people's relationships with technology. This raises the challenge of 'how to situate studies of human–technology relationships in a world where digital data increasingly (albeit differently) compose our environment with the ground underfoot, sky and wind' (Pink and Fors 2017: 386). Here, we likewise call 'for attention beyond the material qualities of the digital/virtual and the affects of human–technology interaction, and towards their often less visible or less obvious co-constituents. It is, we argue, through engaging with this deeper situatedness that we can further understand the contingent and emergent ways of being in the world related to technology design and use' (386).

Above we have carved out a framework for understanding what characterizes learning with data. Different people come to participate in the formation of knowing and meaning through personal data as they live and enact learning in diverse and changing social, historic and material contexts. Thus we understand self-tracking as a 'sensory emplaced learning' practice (Fors, Bäckström and Pink 2013). In the next section we demonstrate the implications of this theoretical framework for how we can understand personal data as a learning resource in our everyday lives.

Learning with data

In this section we examine the reflexive, conscious and unanticipated ways of knowing and learning that develop through the use of contemporary self-tracking technologies and how personal data becomes individual and social knowledge about the body and environment. In contrast to the technically oriented imaginaries discussed above that assume we learn *from* data, we see learning as occurring as an ongoing process. Here learning is not the outcome of a process, rather learning is integral to how we deal with everyday situations and subsequently to how our activities gain meaning for us. In fact, learning is inevitable, and we learn *with* personal data within life-based learning strategies. We build this argument in relation to four dimensions of personal data, each of which offers insights into how and why self-tracking can be an integral part of people's everyday lives: personal data is not completely new information since it is part of what we already tacitly know; it is not static and neutral, it is emergent and continual; it is not detached and objective, but is relational to the situation and environment in which it was produced; and it is not solely cognitively understood, it is also felt.

Personal data is part of what we tacitly know

Non-media-centric media scholars (for example, Moores 2012; Couldry 2012; Pink and Leder Mackley 2013) have urged us to attend not simply to the informational content and communicative affordances of media but to focus on how it becomes part of everyday routines and activities. Similarly, it was not always the technologies themselves or the precision of the data that all our participants were interested in, but the activities and life trajectories in which they become embedded. As we learned from people who showed us how they had abandoned some apps while others were still used, technologies become meaningful in everyday activities and environments in relation to how they are situated, appropriated and improvised with. For such participants, the design intention that these apps would produce neutral data for the user to reflect on and change behaviour accordingly tends to be a problem to be overcome rather than providing new rationalizing insights through which to reach a set goal.

For example, Vaike's encounter with Richard, a media professional who occasionally used self-tracking apps when he felt that he had gained too much weight, shows how this can play out. Richard's overall assessment was that self-tracking was 'meaningless'. However, when he looked through the graphs and visualizations, other aspects of the collected data than the obvious calorie count and timestamps caught his interest. For instance, he showed Vaike an app that tracked his walks by visualizing it on a map, while it showed other data about his physical activity. He described how he found the intended use quite uninteresting, but he dutifully showed how it worked. After scrolling through the graphs and maps he suddenly stopped and started to talk about how the particular map made him remember the walk and what it felt like.

> I use it very randomly, the times I have used it I have mostly listened to audiobooks and walked around – [he stops at one of the registered walks and opens it by clicking on it] you see the result here [pointing at the numbers], sure I can feel some differences bla-bla-bla, but this is what counts as a result. Here are some numbers, it shows I burned 447 calories and that I walked for an hour, 6.5 kilometres, so then you know that. But it does not mean so much. [Scrolling through the maps] Hey, I actually can remember walking this round. I walked around to look at houses, and I walked around in the same block just to see if there were any cool houses and architecture – When I look at the map I remember that specific round.

This 're-discovery' of what the maps in the app actually meant for him, how he used to stroll around the city and looked for cool buildings and architectures, was distorted by how he thought that the app *should* be used to be effective. Despite the fact that he started off the whole conversation about this particular app with stating that this kind of self-tracking was completely 'meaningless' to him, he on the other hand also demonstrated that it became interesting and meaningful when it resonated with his real-world experience of that particular walk and what he already knew through his body. Our next example shows more explicitly how such an incorporation of self-tracking devices and personal data into embodied meaning-making processes becomes intertwined with experiences of the environment, and thus creating new possibilities for sensory emplaced learning processes to unfold. In turn, as we will see in the next example, these processes open up new routes to articulate and understand the tacit and embodied knowing already accumulated through physical activities in different environments.

Magnus was fifty years old and had been wearing a self-tracking wristband for over three years. He had begun using the technology for health reasons. As he explained, he was slightly overweight and suffered from diabetes. He originally hoped that the technology would help motivate him to move a little more and lose weight. In the beginning it did help him in this way, but the weight loss proved to be temporary, which he blamed on the medications he was taking for his diabetes more than anything else. Despite this setback, Magnus remained an avid self-tracker. In fact, when we met him he was wearing two wristbands (one on each arm) and had a third health app on his smartphone. He moved seamlessly between the technologies, writing information about his activities on the smartphone app, as the wristbands measured his steps, pulse and activity level. When asked why he was wearing two wristbands, he explained that he was afraid that the band on his right wrist was about to give up on him, so he bought the second one, a Garmin, in preparation for that day. The problem was that the new wristband did not record his steps as accurately as the old one but had other strengths that he appreciated. He referred to it as his 'golf band'. In addition to registering the strength of his swing, it had a scorecard function that allowed him to register his game and another GPS-based function that informed him of his distance to the green. When Tom asked him if the Garmin actually helped his game, he nodded and replied:

> Yeah, I've learned a lot more about distance than what my clubs tell me, had I just begun by hitting with the clubs. So I've learned, if I hit with this club, I can hit the ball this far. If I take the eight club I can hit thiiiiis far! And that helps me with my golf when I look at my armband and see I have 135 metres to the green. Then I can decide which club to use. So what I used to do by eyeballing it … (laughter) … which I still do sometimes, because they've measured the course but the GPS is plus or minus 4 to 5 metres. Yeah, that's eight metres which it can be off, and that's a club!

By repeatedly comparing the outcome of his use of the golf clubs with the information coming from the Garmin, Magnus learned in part the distance he and his clubs could achieve. In doing so, he made the connections between his embodied knowing and his self-tracking to make these digital and analogue technologies appear to work seamlessly together. The outcome for him was a clearer understanding of what he could achieve with each club in his bag. However, the Garmin did more than provide information to Magnus about his own body, it also enabled him to conceptualize a relationship between his body and the landscape of the golf course around him. It worked as an extension of the sight provided by his eyes as a means of measuring distance, but it did not replace his eyes. To the contrary, Magnus was aware of the limits of the Garmin's GPS to accurately calculate distance, and he consequently constantly weighed the information provided by the technology against his own judgement and calculation of distance, drawn from his embodied experience. In short, the wristband on Magnus's right arm was the tool he trusted to tell him how many steps he had taken and how many calories he had burned. It was a tool that he said could motivate him to take an extra walk around the block if he was a few hundred steps short of his 10,000 set/day goal. The Garmin on his left hand spoke to him about the strength of his golf swing, but it also situated him in the landscape around him, enabled him to understand his place in it and his distance to the geographies around him.

Personal data is emergent and continuous

A study of self-tracking and cycle commuting in the Australian cities of Melbourne and Canberra in 2016, undertaken by Sarah Pink with Shanti Sumartojo, identified among other things the emergent and continuous dimensions of personal data. Research participants repeatedly described how the data they created as they recorded their rides to and from work became crucial to how they understood this routine activity but also their own bodies and physical abilities. The research process involved the participants (eighteen in total) recording their cycle routes on helmet-mounted GoPro cameras and subsequently discussing these with researchers in an interview. The participants' narratives demonstrated how data came to shape how they thought about the routes, distances, speeds and relative achievement of their rides vis-à-vis other riders and their own previous rides; that is, it became part of the way they learned and knew about their bodies and environments over time. At the same time, our discussions with the participants about the GoPro video recordings of their cycling routes that they had made for the research process brought to the fore the embodied and sensory ways of knowing that were similarly constantly generated through this activity. As the digital and material elements of self-tracking were entangled in their rides, their ways of knowing through self-tracking became digital-material (Pink et al. 2016) ways of knowing, reinforced by their engagement with online communities that cohered around sharing data about their rides.

The creation, sharing and understanding of data was part of an ongoing and variable process that was contingent on shifting configurations of elements, including the weather, the season, their bikes, how the riders' bodies felt, the presence of other riders (both on the actual route and in imagined online comparisons) and the possibility that the technologies they used were not working as they expected. Overall, as people self-tracked, space and the movement of their bodies through it came to be conceptualized as datafied, which in turn meant data emerged as contingent, continuing and affective. Together, cycling and self-tracking data were entangled in how people came to know and assess the fitness of their bodies, the physical milestones, challenges and pleasure of their commuting routes, and the activities of other people in their online communities where cycling data were shared.

This was particularly evident in our conversations with participants about 'fitness' and around words such as 'fast' or 'speed', terms that took on relative meanings linked to how data came to define them. For example, Mark defined 'fast' and 'fitness' in terms of his personal data that comprised an important part of what he knew about his rides. This was something cumulative that involved a continuing process of fitness and knowing both through and with the technologies and his body:

Mark: [Self-tracking data are] part of this knowledge that I have that wasn't available ten years ago. Ten years ago, I would have ridden up the hill and thought 'Gee I'm fast,' but these days I get to see how fast I really am. That's motivating for me to try harder and get faster and fitter. This [self-tracking commuting] is a way of seeing how I'm going as times goes by, and it being a daily sort of race rather than just every month I go to an event and race.

| *Interviewer:* | If you didn't have the data to confirm that you were fit, would you feel as fit? |
| *Mark:* | I'd feel less confident in how I was feeling. Certainly it would make me question it a bit more. I'd still feel good but wouldn't have that confirmation, wouldn't feel as confident about how I'd do in a race or whatever. When I feel I'm on that trajectory [of getting fitter], heading upwards, it just confirms it. |

The meaning of Mark's data emerged in a sort of dialogue with his sense of his body, as he checked how he 'felt' with information about his speed, distance, elevation and heart rate recorded by his self-tracking devices and bike computer. This checking and rechecking was a lively conversation that saw the data shape his confidence and motivation in a continuing and constantly changing fashion. The pedagogical nature of Mark's personal data required his constant evaluation and re-evaluation, based on his previous experiences with his data. Even though he learnt how to evaluate his 'performance' through this process, he still felt the data confirmed what he might otherwise have known from how tired his body felt. His data were thus inextricable from the physical and affective aspects of his riding and worked powerfully on how he approached his commutes and how he imagined he would perform on future rides or races. The digital materiality and corporeality of such ways of knowing in movement shows how such contingent and continual shifting knowing emerges from self-tracking activities. It is not therefore a type of knowledge that is already existing and that can be applied by self-trackers to interpret their activity or to motivate them towards fitness. Instead, such knowledge relies on how data emerges as part of physical movement.

Personal data is part of our lived environments

As we have discussed in Chapter 2, in many parts of the world our everyday environments are now constituted and rendered knowable through various engagements with data, which through self-tracking technologies are made apparent to us through representational categories, including data visualizations, sound alerts and vibrations which we feel on our skin. Thus, as digital data becomes increasingly ubiquitous, self-tracking becomes a way for us to situate ourselves sensorially, emotionally and representationally within this wider quantified world. For instance, it is often not just elements of our movement that are tracked but, rather, that the personal data that refers to the movement of our bodies is tracked in relation to other data. An example of this is when people use apps that track their daily activity; this is often represented on maps, thus bringing together personal movement with data relating to GPS and location and mapping. Therefore we do not simply track ourselves but we track ourselves in a datafied world (Pink and Fors 2017). Meeting Chris Dancy, who we introduced in Chapter 1, after we had developed these ideas was exciting because Chris's work seemed to account for these relationships from both technological and affective perspectives. Referring to his understanding of the layering of the different elements that make up our everyday worlds, Chris explained to Sarah how he understood the spatial situatedness of data:

> To me when I think about my data and my life I think about it a lot like a Google map so you know if you just go to Google maps on the web you usually start above a location somewhere to where you're at with about a 20 to 30 mile radius from there you can actually tag on satellite view you can toggle on traffic, you can toggle on other things and … as you reveal those layers you, more is interested and more is there for you to understand … what's going on, if it's night time it actually inverts the colours it shows to the same depth, through the prism of day or night, but then if you zoom in you start getting more depth, so you get not just big building names but big street names and then little street names and if you zoom in far enough you actually go into street view where you go down on that level … so for me what good is the data if you can't start out big and reveal you know, those layers.

The proliferation of sensor technologies and modes of engaging with data that Chris has developed gives his home some characteristics of a smart home. However, the focus on the data that he collects from and through his home is directed towards his understanding of his own relationship with his environment rather than simply increasing the efficient running of the home. Moreover, like his self-tracking, the ways in which he has made his home smart do not follow the conventional modes of smart-home design but, rather, have created a home that is intelligent in the ways that he needs it to be and that he can control in the ways he wishes. This kind of improvisatory activity that goes beyond the intended uses of designed objects or technologies is, as we show in Chapter 6, often characteristic of technology design and use.

Chris Dancy's use and design of new self-tracking technologies, sensors and apps demonstrates the possibilities of what humans can do with the new technologies that are emerging, as we are on the cusp of what is being touted as a new step in the automation of many aspects of our lives and societies. Chris's use of tracking technologies also makes it possible to know the human body in ways that were formerly impossible; however, his example is also significant because his mode of tracking situates the human body in relation to multiple elements of the environments in which people live and with which they interact as they live out their everyday lives. In this sense his approach coincides with our theoretical and empirical interest in the situatedness of self-tracking, and our understanding of data as representing not simply the activities of the body in question but rather as being emergent from the relationship between that particular body and the specific – but continually changing – environmental configuration of which it is a part at any one moment.

Personal data is felt

As such, if we consider personal data as part of the environments we are *in* rather than simply representational visualizations of body activity that we look *at,* we can think of data as being 'felt'. We found that it was felt by participants in our research in two ways. First, people use data to make themselves feel comfortable in the world, for instance, through everyday routines or 'data practices' and through the relationships they make between their bodies and their data. Second, people find or seek ways to feel comfortable about how their data are or may be shared or used in the world (i.e. by companies with rights over the data and by third parties). However, data can also feel un/ comfortable in situations that are not shared. For our participants, data were felt and were experienced as part of wider social and physical environments, which in turn generated feelings of meaningfulness and meaninglessness. For instance, Richard, who we met in the example above discussing his sense of meaninglessness when self-tracking, compared it with playing the card game

Patience with yourself, 'sometimes it works out and sometimes it doesn't, nobody cares'. His stories about when and where his self-tracking devices came into play in his routines clearly connected to when his data felt comfortable and when they did not. One example was the way Richard sometimes used his Weight Watchers app to gather information on what he ate and subsequently how much he was allowed to eat according to the app if he wanted to lose weight (which was the main reason he initially started monitoring his food). When he was asked about when and why he stopped food-intake tracking, his answer showed that this decision was closely connected to experiences of comfort. It also revealed how the data gathering is related to not only a feeling of knowing but to knowing much more about yourself than you want to make visible.

> I stopped [food tracking] when I started to cheat too much. For example, I think I just drank three beers yesterday evening, so I registered that and not the five [beers] I actually drank. It is on that level, you know. It is worse to see here [pointing at the app] that I cheat than to know that I cheat. I know it, but I don't need to register it in the app, tell the app that I am cheating.

The data in Richard's app made him stop monitoring his food intake, not because of what the information represented in terms of facts and figures but in terms of how his experiential response to the data-collection practice made him feel uncomfortable with what his cheating made him learn about himself. His way to describe how 'it is worse to see here [in the app] that I cheat than to know that I cheat' suggests how this feeling turned his attention to otherwise tacit and unspoken aspects of himself. The affective/emotional category comfort turns here into a learning resource through the use of food-monitoring apps.

An example of how the feeling of comfort instead can become a pivotal point for maintaining and creating opportunities for personal sense-making in food tracking is shown by Jens, who we introduced in the introduction of this chapter. Jens describes how his food tracking has been entangled with stress management when working at home. In a situation where he described how he had to work late at home to meet a deadline, which was a recurring situation in his work life, food tracking had become part of how he made that situation 'feel good'. He began the story with telling us about how he used to eat candy when he had to work late to keep going, even if he was tired:

> I have a scale in our kitchen. I took four pieces of candy and put them on the scale: OK it was 15 g. And then I put the candy beside my computer and then I registered them in my app. Then I put the candy to the side to be able to continue working. I saved them so I had them when I worked. This control makes me feel so good … Then I ate them one at the time because I value it much more.

Together these examples show how *comfort* can be explained as more than a feeling that comes from collecting personal data, and as emerging learning resource through which self-tracking and personal data accrue meaning for users.

Conclusion

We contend that learning to live with one's personal data is a form of pedagogical work, inciting and demanding reflection on how useful, valid or valuable these data may be, and to what extent they should be incorporated into concepts of selfhood and embodiment. As we have shown through our empirical examples, self-tracking cannot be analysed in isolation from the details of how data is activated through sensory, emotional and emplaced learning processes.

The ethnographic approach taken in these studies invites us to account for the experience of living in a world of personal data, identifying the ways in which these data become constituted and incorporated into everyday life as part of routine practices. We have argued that we need to move beyond simplistic ideas of personal data as neutral bearers of information for people to reflect upon and thereby change their behaviours to address flaws and move away from less beneficial ways of doing things. We also suggested that more cognitive- and technology-centred ideas of how people use and make meaning of personal data neglect the various ways that the body in its social and physical environment is part of how personal data become meaningful in people's everyday lives. In our ambitions to embrace these embodied and emplaced dimensions of how people learn to live in a world where digital personal data is part of their habits and routines, we introduced a way of thinking about data not as merely facts to process cognitively but as something that is attributed with meaning through embodied and emplaced pedagogies that emerge through the way data become part of people's lives. In our empirical examples we show how these pedagogies, and the routes to knowing they imply, are played out and materialized in different everyday situations. In these diverse examples some aspects of learning become evident when looking at them through our theoretical lens that might be easy to overlook from other perspectives since they adhere to the unarticulated, invisible and non-representational in everyday life. Nevertheless, they are vital parts of what self-tracking brings to our attention.

Our examples show how the pedagogies through which data is given everyday meanings are characterized by three components:

Self-tracking technologies add to and alter embodied experiences. Our examples show that the data-producing technologies are not invisible lenses on activity, their presence is felt through how they become part of bodily sensations of otherwise unspoken or unarticulated feelings.

Data feels something not in itself but as part of an environment (physical or imagined). Therefore, the meanings associated with personal data are not invoked simply by numbers. Figures and graphs are not necessarily the main learning resource. The people in our examples made sense of the data in relation to the way data was connected to activities and its environment.

Data configures and construes unspoken and unanticipated dimensions of knowing. The presence of sensors, apps and data does not imply rational ways of thinking or afford structured self-reflections cognitively. From the moment somebody puts on a self-tracking device or decides to start to register personal data in an app, it starts to invoke feelings, intertwine with habits, become implicated in ways of looking, and disturb and describe mundane activities.

Yet, personal data may be alternatively ignored, disregarded or resisted, deemed as lacking interest or value or as inciting negative emotions. The different examples we have discussed illustrate these heterogeneous affective, embodied and experiential dimensions of how people live with data. They demonstrate that the use of devices that produce personal data are imbued with, or attached to, not only sensory, embodied and affective categories but also how these sensory categories are entangled with the technologies that registered the data and the social and physical environment in which the data made sense. They are learning resources which orient users' attention and sensemaking to the non-representational and experiential aspects of learning to know themselves rather than principally to the data as content and information.

6

Anticipatory Data Worlds

In this chapter we examine how futures are imagined through self-tracking and personal data. These devices, platforms and data are bound up in a contemporary societal moment that Adams, Murphy and Clarke characterize as being in a 'state of anticipation, of thinking and living toward the future' (2009: 246). They are also implicated in how ordinary people imagine their own futures. As we have shown in Chapters 4 and 5, self-tracking technologies have certain ways of 'thinking' about the temporalities of human action, but people often do not necessarily use them as these logics demand. Here, we explore further how different but related possible futures of self-tracking are articulated and produced in everyday life, and organizational and research environments. We first discuss the anticipatory modes that emerged as people who frequently used self-tracking devices over time learned with their personal data. We next discuss how people involved with professional organizations and non-profit communities, for whom self-tracking crosses the personal and professional areas of their lives, as designer-users, envision the future of self-tracking. Then we reflect on how future but not yet marketed self-tracking and personal data emerge through groundbreaking emerging technologies.

Conceptualizing futures

Future is a contested term and, as we established in Chapter 1, we are not concerned with predicting short- or long-term futures as technology marketing, policy-makers and insurance companies may be. For such organizations the future is a projected moment into which they might invest financially or through other efforts in the present, in order to reach expected benefits or targets at a time that has not yet happened. Self-tracking technologies, wearables and their future iterations are like any technology discussed in terms of their predicted future share value on financial markets. For example, 'The global fitness tracker market' is understood as a growing market and 'is expected to reach approximately USD 15.88 billion by the end of 2023', which has been attributed to 'growing adoption of technology, rising popularity towards smart gadgets and benefits of fitness trackers' (Market Research Future 2019). Sturken and Thomas (2004) suggest that new technologies have a tendency to become a canvas for people to project and stage what they believe are contemporary urgent future issues. As explained in Chapter 4, the self-tracking technologies market is characterized by an anticipatory mode that proposes a healthy, fit and active future, and corresponds with a design logic that follows the 'self-improvement hypothesis' discussed in Chapter 5. In this 'culture of anticipation' (Panchasi 2009), people's meaning-making with emerging technologies becomes an arena where possible futures are negotiated. The historian Roxanne Panchasi suggests that how the future is anticipated at a particular historical moment 'can tell us a great deal about the cultural preoccupations and political perspectives of the *present doing the anticipation*' (2009: 4). In policy contexts and through their relationship with technologically driven digital health research the expectation that self-tracking technologies might bring about 'behaviour change' that will help to fix societal problems related to health, such as obesity, heart problems and other conditions associated with lack of exercise or unregulated exercise, is presented as a possible 'solution' to future health problems that are predicted to have human and economic costs. Indeed, insurance companies are well known, and by some feared, for incorporating digital health tracking into their policies, in ways that invest in future health (Lupton 2016a: 122–123).

Our approach to and definition of futures runs against such conceptualizations of futures as defined, predicted and knowable. A future anthropologies approach emphasizes the impossibility of knowing futures (Pink and Salazar 2017) and that 'our futures are contingent because our present is as well' (Bessire and Bond 2014: 450). As shown in Chapter 5, the ways in which self-tracking and personal data play out are contingent on the everyday life circumstances in which they are embedded rather than being independent from and *impacting on* contemporary everyday lives. As Pink and Salazar (2017) summarize: 'Future worlds will likewise be emergent, but constituted through different configurations of things, processes and the contingencies that are part of them', and thus future self-tracking and personal data will be equally embedded in these complexities of as yet unknown futures. Therefore we conceptualize futures through the notion of possibility. The possible offers us a way to understand the future as populated by convincing scenarios that continue the threads of the past and present, yet which we cannot be sure will happen.

The anticipatory modes of everyday self-tracking

When we began researching self-tracking and personal data, one of our central interests was in how people imagined their own personal and bodily futures, and the futures of self-tracking technologies and personal data. We wondered if participants would use their data and goal setting to envisage a future body or experience, if they saw their self-tracking as related to their future health, relationships with healthcare institutions and professionals or insurance companies, and what kinds of wearables or bio-tracking devices they imagined they would use in the future. As discussed in Chapter 5, we also pondered whether participants who did not use these technologies as future-oriented behaviour change tools were disappointed that the hope that they would impact on their future health or fitness was not played out over time. In fact, we found that the extent and ways in which participants engaged with the future temporalities of self-tracking were commensurate with their existing interest in and ways of learning with self-tracking and personal data. Thus, while for some people certain anxieties about their data futures informed how they engaged with self-tracking technologies and personal data in the present, others imagined futures in which these concerns would be negligible.

For example, Christof, who was based in Australia and ran his own small company, was a long-term and committed self-tracker, who tracked many areas of his life including steps, sleep and heart rate, as well as connecting his tracking to his Google Calendar and other accounts. He was also interested in, and had been involved with, the QS Movement. Christof was interested in how tracking many of his activities could participate in his future, but he was not concerned that collecting and sharing his personal data could impact negatively on his future. This was partly because he understood his data as having a future-focused element that was personalized to him in ways that constituted how he felt comfortable with his data. He explained how he aggregated some of this data using Google Calendar, which he had used to record his 'personal story' for around fifteen years when we met. He felt comfortable in relation to the control he maintained of his own data, because, as he described it: 'by using so many tools and navigating that, I'm the only one who knows how to navigate that space'. Thus he felt his data was disparate and not accessible to any one organization as a whole, telling Sarah that 'it's not in one central repository', rather it was located across a range of different platforms. Therefore, he explained that, for him, while 'people talk about the permanence of data ... this idea that once you put something on the internet it's always there it will never be forgotten. This is really false ... it's a needle in haystack scenario'. He acknowledged celebrities might well become the targets of hackers, this was not the case 'when it comes to my future and myself'. He moreover believed external users of his data were uninterested in any specificities or differences between himself and other users, seeing platforms as being interested in 'population patterns, not the personal narratives'. Thus he felt that he benefited from accessing and 'actively managing' his personal narrative, because he was the only person who could make sense of it. As he described it, because he was in control of his present self, 'no one can come along and ... manipulate my future self'. Thus, the way that he managed his tracking enabled him to feel that he had a foot in the future, which helped him to secure his future personal and career trajectories. Christof's use of self-tracking and personal data was extensive; however; his views were echoed in our research with other participants. For instance, another participant, who likewise used several different platforms, told Sarah that 'Fitbit almost feels like, maybe it's getting a quarter of the story, but it's an easily measured quarter of the story, then all the measurements [which I might do manually] are another part of the story, and then there's the ... Fitness Test [a digital online fitness programme that I participate in with a friend, that uses a different platform] that's kind of another part'. The idea that one's personal data is dispersed and that indeed the personal aspect of it is only available to the individual who aggregates it themselves provided these participants with reassurance that they were sufficiently in control of their data in the present and that therefore sharing it would not lead them to any harm in the future. Each participant developed a particular logic through which to ensure that they felt comfortable with the ways that they engaged with personal data, whether like these participants it involved particular understandings of the world of data and commercial interests they were attached to, or if like another participant they used multiple email accounts to join different platforms. Most did not have clear visions of what self-tracking meant for their personal futures, and while they discussed with us the possibilities of it becoming implicated in their future healthcare reviews, planning or diagnosis with their medical doctors, and mulled over the question of if it would or would not be beneficial for their health insurer to access such data, such questions did not appear to be central to their future imaginaries of their lives with self-tracking and personal data.

Our research also showed that, even when their initial motive for self-tracking might have resonated with goal-oriented purposes to lose weight, get fit or feel better, over time our participants' aspirations changed along with the meaning self-tracking held for them. When people discovered if and how self-tracking contributed to their existing activities and imaginaries, their aspirations for it changed accordingly. For example, Eva, an experienced self-tracker, told Vaike that it was not primarily an urge to change herself that inspired her to self-track. Instead, when the technology was introduced in Sweden, she was interested in how it could assist her professionally as a physical education teacher. She was seeking an alternative to scenarios where she had to tell teenagers that they had unhealthy lifestyles, through a digital tool that opened up technological possibilities for the teenagers themselves to start to experiment with their personal data. She had no expectations that they would straightforwardly change their behaviours. Instead, her ambition was simply to make them aware of how their lives appeared through digital representation and thus to enable them to understand themselves in new ways that resonated with their digital lives outside of school.

Eva also had a very physically active life herself, and when she started to experiment with self-tracking devices as tools for teaching she also started to digitally track her own activities with the same intentions. She has continually and frequently used her run tracking app, not so much to register pace and distance but to use the GPS data visualizations on the app's map to analyse how well 'the inner body watch and body compass match with what the technology presents'. She explained that the visualizations made it possible to go through her runs afterwards – the pace, topography and distance – and then make sense of how that matched her memories. If the map did not match her experience, she favoured her experience and memory.

When she demonstrated to Vaike how she went through her maps, she described it as 're-living the run' and that she 'sat and played with it [the map] … I can think about "what happened here" [pointing at a position on the map]'. In this example she was looking, or rather feeling, through a run during which she had accompanied and aided a visually impaired person, with whom she was planning to run a marathon. Eva continued:

Figure 6.1 Eva shows her routine of 'feeling through' her personal data produced during a trail run, re-enacting not only how the run went in terms of physical achievements but also how it felt to run in that particular setting with her specific companions. Photo: Vaike Fors.

We were out running here [pointing at the map]. It was 20 kilometres, it can be good to save the map so I know until next time … but this [pointing at measurements like step counts and longest runs] I don't care about. I already know that I have been running longer distances. Look, I added an extra loop at the end … and I remember that she fell up here. I know exactly where she fell, she fell at mark number 14 [pointing at a marker on the map] because it was uphill and I didn't remember to tell her to be careful that it was slippery.

Eva's use of self-tracking devices was not framed by a goal-oriented anticipation of her future fitness or health. Instead, her continuous self-tracking was deeply entangled in the embodied knowing she developed through her different physical activities. When Vaike asked her how she imagined she would use the personal data she produced through self-tracking in the future, Eva described how she always wore her smartwatch and looked through her data from time to time, but in parallel with all the apps that track her physical activity she kept a written diary where she wrote her experience of her well-being. Approximately five days a week, she would document if she was happy, sad, satisfied, frustrated and so on. This started long before digital versions of diaries were available, but now she created these diary notes through an app. Sometimes she added photos and she reflected on how differently she read this diary in comparison to her activity trackers. In the former she never sought out patterns in her past experiences, as she sometimes did with the latter. Instead, she sometimes picked up her well-being diary to read a random page, think back to what had happened since then and reflect on why she had described her day like that. Eva also gave the password to her digital diary to her family in case she 'died in a car accident or had a heart attack', even though she warned them to read it at their own risk because it is not always happy reading. She wanted them to be able to read it even though it was not written for anyone else to read. Like Eva, Christof also spoke with Sarah about his interest in archiving the mundane in everyday life and the sense of well-being that he gained from this. He related how he liked tracking his GPS location using the moves app, because it helped to jog his memory. As he described it, this app automatically tracked his GPS location all day, counted his steps and the number of kilometres he covered, which meant he would not need to check in with the app when he arrived somewhere, because it tracked where he went automatically. This data was important for him because, he said, 'I can get an aggregate for how far I have walked' and because it showed the parts of the city he spent most time in. It formed part of an archive that he would be able to dip into in the future, as he put it: 'somehow through these apps I'll have a set up that's like a perfect journal' so 'I could replay a day in my mind … things move by so quickly that I like to track them'.

These stories of how people use personal data in self-tracking apps as means to dip into the experience of being somewhere, while doing and feeling something in the past, is a recurring theme through our research. Rather than anticipating that they will change their behaviour by using the app, they experience the app as a tool to explore routines from new perspectives and angles. Checking into one's personal data with this in mind becomes a routine that is embedded in other digital habits. For instance, Josefine demonstrated to Vaike how she named every run that was registered in her app so that she could easily remember its time and place. Afterwards she would go through the list created by her app to relive the feeling of the runs. Even though she saw herself as 'a very goal-focused person', during the interview she realized that that she did not only pay attention to how her personal data showed her progress in reaching her distance and steps goals but that also reading the log made her re-enact the feeling of well-being she experienced during certain runs, and how these feelings were connected to her and her husband's joint running routines. Josefine reflected:

> There are so many feelings connected to it [running data] I talked about it with my husband yesterday, we only ran five kilometres yesterday in a very slow pace, and it's a challenge for me not to think that I should run 10 kilometres because my body can't handle it – then we ran on a trail and we started to talk about how we had felt when we had run this trail before. Somehow there are so many feelings attached to it [the trail], the smells, how it felt physically, it's like a kind of euphoria for me. I can drive past somewhere and start thinking about how it felt when I was running a lot, how then I ran here and then turned back, and I know I have been driving my car here and it feels really far away, and there are a lot of lovely feelings and memories attached to that experience that come back to me when I go back into the statistics [in the app] – and in the history. There are no feelings attached to sitting on an exercise bike in a gym but there are totally different feelings attached to places, smells, time when the elderflowers every year in a particular place and the feel of that smell, I can still evoke that feeling because it is charged with so much positive energy.

On the one hand, it is through these routines that data becomes part of bodily knowing. On the other, however, and what we want to emphasize here, is a particular mode of anticipation that is demonstrated through our examples; as people anticipate becoming more familiar with their routines by re-enacting activities not as behaviours but as part of their sensory experiences of situations and environments that they enjoy and that make them feel good.

In sum, amongst these everyday users, self-tracking and personal data were future-focused in a different way to what we had imagined. They were also different from the future-focused modes of use represented in the logics of the discourses of marketing and technology design discussed in Chapter 4. The mode of anticipatory practice they involved formed part of the ways people lived and learned with self-tracking and personal data, which we discussed in Chapter 5. These participants were concerned with the meanings self-tracking data held for them in the day-to-day present, as they incrementally learned with their technologies. They often anticipated going 'backwards' through data in their own futures, to relive not only the feeling of the activity but also what happened, what that meant to them then and how it felt to remember it. Furthermore, this mode of anticipation developed through the ongoing use of the devices. This less-visible mode of anticipation runs parallel with more explicit training and well-being goals, whereby participants felt themselves to be in familiar routines that encompassed the temporality of past, present and future. In doing so they learned about themselves *with* the data rather than *from* the graphs and visualizations, and it did not seem to bother them that the apps did not provide them with what they had anticipated when they started to use it according to the built-in design intentions. Knowing that the data they tracked in the immediate present would directly slip over into the past, they 'saved' that past for future contemplation. However, rather than being associated with tangible future goals or to mitigate anxieties about particular future scenarios, this anticipatory mode was set within the comfort of familiar daily, weekly or other known temporal routines through which learning and knowing incrementally come about.

In the next section we describe our encounters with a team of developers behind a device that, according to the developers, could create a better life by logging your activities without the ambition to change behaviours in a particular direction. In Chapter 4 we focused on technology development that is based in anticipation of a better life through behavioural change. In the following section we will discuss how a self-tracking device built on somewhat other logics, more aligned with ideas to capture everyday realities for people to dip into and rediscover how their everyday life can look.

Designing to rediscover the present in the future

The Narrative clip, introduced in Chapter 4, is a small wearable camera that you clip on your clothes, which, according to its website, will help you to 'live the moment while effortlessly capturing it' (Narrative n.d.). Its developers described it as providing a 'photographic memory' with minimal effort by taking a high-resolution photo every 30 seconds, thus capturing everything that is in front of the wearer without discrimination. Every two days or less, the photos are uploaded to the Narrative database to be stored and processed by algorithms that group them together in moments and elevate the best ones automatically. Vaike and Martin's interview with the owner and the lead developers of this life-logging technology suggests that they imagine the Narrative Clip as a device that can capture the authenticity of the world in which the user is situated. The human actor becomes a spectator in everyday life and is assumed to relinquish the situated and subjective gaze through which they interpret and imagine the technologies and images being used. This approach to the camera invokes an idea of everyday life whereby its fleeting 'magical' moments are recordable, re-liveable, re-presented and remembered (Fors, Berg and Pink 2016).

These ideas, which also differ from the goal-oriented anticipation of a better life discussed in Chapter 4, are rooted in the developer's own experience of self-tracking. Martin, the owner of the company that developed the Narrative Clip, told Martin and Vaike how his personal story inspired him to develop the device:

> My whole life I have wished to document my life. I don't know where that urge came from … and I wanted to do it simpler and more automated to remember things without putting a lot of effort into the documentation in itself [with a camera] … I have lost both of my parents to cancer at different times. And when I look into photo albums that are created to keep the

memories from the times I spent with them, it only captures the good times. It is when you are happy and open presents together, and the weather is nice when you went on excursions. Very few of the mundane moments when you sit and eat your cereal in the morning are in these albums. Or when it is raining outside and it was boring and you sat and read a book instead. But these moments are as valuable and important. Even more important than when you actually lived together. I will never get my parents back and the memories are fading ... and this was the starting point for this project, when I actually realised that we could produce a camera that was small enough to wear.

The developers strove to create a device through which people could visually log their lives and later scroll through their days, reviewing the things they had done and the people they met. The developers believed that by reminding people of their day the device would augment how they treasured the people they knew and the things they had achieved. Thus, their motto was 'for moments that matter', and they anticipated a future where people could 'save, or capture, visual memories while staying present in the moment'; thus representing a mode of anticipation more aligned with how everyday self-trackers hope their personal data will give them new perspectives on everyday routines.

In the next section we discuss how researchers who are also experienced self-trackers and forerunners in the non-profit community Quantified Self (QS) discuss these issues and how they anticipate the future direction of contemporary self-tracking.

'Apps suck – they are created for solutions in search for problems'

In seeking participants with extensive experience of self-tracking, we contacted people connected with the QS community in the Nordic countries. In part QS has become a metaphor for a diverse cluster of self-tracking cultures fuelled by a range of incentives, spanning from market-oriented discourse (Ruckenstein and Pantzar 2017), to resistance of dominant interests (Nafus and Sherman 2014) and a variety of practices (see, for example, Lupton 2016b; and Nafus 2016). The practices of particular group of experienced Nordic QS self-trackers we engaged with differed from those of the everyday self-trackers discussed above but can equally be understood through a learning approach. The experienced QS-oriented self-trackers we met had developed ways to incrementally learn *with* their technologies but not in the service of self-improvement according to pre-set goals. Instead, the goal is processual, meaning that they contemplated how their self-tracking could open new routes to learn more about their bodies, how it works and how it responds to different ways of doing things. This mode of anticipation developed through their ongoing use of the devices. However, since the QS members we met were veterans in this field, their ways of anticipating future self-tracking were simultaneously part of an agenda to change not only the way self-tracking devices could be developed but also, on an institutional level, how self-tracking could change the underlying ideas of how to perform healthcare. Thus revealing their visions of the future of self-tracking itself, and how they anticipated that future technologies could feed their personal self-tracking aspirations and how they might learn with them into their own futures.

The QS forum is full of individuals seeking advice relating to apps that will increase their cognitive abilities, measure personal values and track calories (Quantified Self 2015), all of which merit a reflection over the degree to which technology guides individuals and in the process deprives them of agency. However, viewing self-tracking networks such as QS from perspectives that are all too technologically deterministic in nature runs the risk of failing to appreciate the fact that there is more at stake here than issues of discipline, power and people being blindly steered by the allure of new technologies. The QS and other self-tracking networks alike are not only early adopters but in many cases they also participate in the processes of developing new tracking technologies based on what they have learned through their own self-tracking activities. These activities might presage activities that a broader public may take up later and thus make visible future technological possibilities and provide opportunities for insights into how new self-tracking developments might be steered in ethical and sustainable directions. As Pantzar, Ruckenstein and Mustonen (2017) remind us, new self-tracking technologies allow methodological innovation and experimentation, and longitudinal QS-inspired self-tracking can be seen as setting up "a laboratory of the self" where people co-evolve with technologies' (Brogård Kristensen and Ruckenstein 2018: 1). In Chapter 1 we discussed the One Button Tracker, presented by the QS veterans Thomas Blomseth Christiansen and Jakob Eg Larsen, as being developed to allow for 'active tracking' – a way of 'noticing things from the inside'. The device deviated from the high-tech self-tracking market, since it allowed for a shift in modes of anticipation: instead of preparing people for imagining a future improved self in terms of fitness, it was designed to focus on how the body felt and functioned in the present and to track only what people cared about today. The outcome was up to the user to define. By highlighting the open-endedness and future uncertainties of self-tracking, Blomseth Christiansen and Eg Larsen discussed how the One Button Tracker 'questioned the behaviourist and market-based underpinnings of contemporary self tracking design'.

Experienced self-trackers at the core of the Nordic QS community likewise understood and experimented with self-tracking technologies as *pedagogical* tools, also following this mode of anticipation based in open-ended self-experimentation. For instance, in Stockholm, Vaike met with Henrik and Sara, who were two of the co-founders of QS Stockholm, the local meet-up group, in 2012, straight after Sara had been to the first QS conference in Europe. Henrik emphasized the experimental, experiential and subjective character of what he called 'the QS-method':

> It is to investigate yourself, follow, test, log, and evaluate what works for me. The QS-method is to find general, smart ways of doing all that. This is why so much of QS services are smartphone-based. These are the things that will be become future healthcare too. It has to be simple and as automated as possible, otherwise it won't work.

Henrik continued speaking about how important the self-guided exploration was, seeing each person as 'their own focus group', and emphasized two key points:

> Firstly, I can learn to learn about myself. Secondly, I have to acknowledge that my insights might not be applicable to others. That is an insight in itself. That not all people are like me. And that is why it is fun to share stories [in the QS community].

While Henrik still was engaged in QS Stockholm, Sara had dropped out because she did not find it interesting to focus on the gadgets:

The QS from the outside is a lot of technology which for me is not interesting at all. It is not the apps that are engaging, it is what you can do with them that interests me … That is why I am not engaging in QS Stockholm anymore – it became too superficial and was all about gadgets.

Sara's own career as a PhD student in health informatics is based in her work on self-care in Parkinson's Disease, in which she studies her own self-tracking. She has become a well-known blogger and presenter, and activist when it comes to patient-centred healthcare. On her web page she describes her self-tracking:

The other part of the title: 'self-tracking' is probably less familiar, even though I am sure that some of you readers have some sort of perception of what 'self-tracking' might entail. I am guessing that most of you then think of gadgets and devices, cool-looking technology, often used by ultra-runners, long-distance cyclists and other people seldom associated with Parkinson's or other chronic conditions.

I will not pretend that I don't appreciate technology, anyone who knows me even slightly would immediately call my bluff. I'll be honest: I LOVE gadgets, devices, technology in every form! But, to me, self-tracking is so much more than technology. Self-tracking is, in my opinion, the most powerful weapon I can wish for in my battle against Parkinson's and I will explain why. I see my neurologist once or twice a year, about half-an-hour every time. That is one hour per year, and the rest of the year's 8,765 hours, I spend in selfcare. I am sure it is the same way for a lot of you out there as well. This means that I am directly in contact with healthcare's practises and clinical guidelines for my Parkinson's during no more than one hour per year. And it is only during this one hour that my neurologist can assess my symptoms, observe how my condition progresses and evaluate my status. It is also during this one hour per year that my treatment is being prescribed, different medications and other interventions. But it is during the rest of the year's 8,765 hours, that I implement the treatment. Because, let's be honest, my neurologist doesn't even know if I take the medications he prescribes. But, probably most important, it is during the 8,765 hours in selfcare that I can observe the effects of the treatment. And this is where self-tracking comes in. (Riggare n.d.)

In her interview with Vaike, Sara returned frequently to the fact that self-tracking is subjective and has to enable one to learn from personal data. The heading for this section is a quote from our interviews: 'Apps sucks – they are created for solutions in search for problems.' It sums up how Sara imagined the future of self-tracking would move beyond technologically oriented and determined solutions and instead focus on how to rethink the production of personal data. She concluded:

> Technology is so much about make up problems to the solutions that the devices are developed to solve – You have to know the problems you want to solve and it takes knowledge rather than measuring, skills rather than technology, and intuition. And it takes courage to follow your own path.

Sara is seen as a forerunner when it comes to taking responsibility of her self-care; she started her project by learning to know how her body felt when she was going to take her medication. She said that she realized that 'it is not [only] an intellectual process – it is part of developing your intuition and gut feeling', where the act of tracking is an essential part of the work of registering. She suggested that the future of self-tracking lies in the idea that people have to take their time to learn experientially, in that 'you have to hang around with your data' to get to know your own problem, instead of following the lead of what commercial self-tracking devices are designed for. She concluded that in this way self-tracking 'becomes rawer, more naked and it takes courage, because you are alone [with your data]'. In this discussion Sara told Vaike that she believed that there was an ongoing shift in the QS community in relation to how the core project was defined. She described how her first year in the QS was all about 'data' and how that had moved to 'information' and later 'knowledge'. The discussion now was centred on how to conceptualize 'knowing' as something that emphasized intuition and skills over measurements and technology. Sara's line of reasoning about future self-tracking is aligned with the One Button Tracker we discussed in Chapter 1, and above. The One Button Tracker focuses on the act of tracking and the relevance of the subjective experience for learning from your data (see also Eg Larsen, Eskelund and Blomseth Christiansen 2017; Pantzar and Ruckenstein 2017). This implies a mode of anticipation that prepares the user to allow for new bodily understandings about things they care about in unpredictable ways. In Sara's case, these forms of embodied knowing gave her courage to contest the dominant belief systems that underpin institutional healthcare.

In this section we have discussed the approaches to the futures of prominent self-trackers. Such people are often consciously active in imagining and designing future technologies and ways of using them that question contemporary design worlds. This includes a shift in modes of anticipation from the pre-set goal-oriented idea of imagining a future improved and normatively fit body, into unpredictable and open-ended self-exploration to find new ways to solve bodily problems that matter for the user. We next focus in on how a range of self-tracking experts more directly envisaged the future of self-tracking.

Envisioning future self-tracking

In Chapter 1 we introduced a design workshop on future self-tracking that we organized with experienced self-trackers, developers, designers and experts in related fields, in Sweden in November 2017, entitled 'Future Learning with Digital Health Service Design.' The workshop aimed to identify ways to disrupt current designs for self-tracking and health services. It discussed how the next generation self-tracking device designs might appear and function differently if the purpose and practice of their use was understood through alternative principles. The workshop included a Post-it session in which we collected future visions in terms of learning and skills, equality, technology, ownership, legal and regulatory issues, societal values and demographics for future digital self-tracking and health service design (Figure 6.2).

After an exercise, where we experienced the 'active self-tracking' offered by Blomseth Christiansen and Eg Larsen's One Button Tracker methodology, we clustered a set of Post-its created earlier into new themes (Figure 6.2). The group agreed that these new themes questioned several strong concepts and abstract principles that underpinned contemporary self-tracking services. For example, through a discussion of the example of machine learning and predictability, the group determined that we need to rethink the increasingly entangled joint human–machine learning that is emerging as measuring technologies become increasingly automated and ubiquitous, and is structuring how self-tracking and personal data can be imagined in a more unarticulated and concealed way. If we do not intervene, then future self-tracking might use

Figure 6.2 Collecting future visions for self-tracking. Photo: Vaike Fors.

predictive, goal-oriented modes of anticipation and remain insensitive to the open-ended and improvisatory nature of self-experimentation that forms the basis of both novice and expert self-tracking.

Therefore, we argue that future self-tracking has to be more sensitive to what happens in everyday lives beyond the scope of what it is designed for to reconcile both what digital self-tracking is programmed for achieving *and* how people improvise with them as they become part of everyday routines. Self-tracking devices are increasingly being developed with algorithms through which the device will accumulate information about the users' whereabouts and activities and 'learn' from them to bring out more individualized feedback in order to reach pre-set goals. Simultaneously, people do not necessarily use them to achieve future-focused goals. Therefore, feedback that results from machine learning might risk missing the target since the users' self-tracking activities are not in a straightforward way based in the same linear goal-oriented logic that the devices are programmed for registering and giving feedback to. In the workshop we concluded that to push the self-tracking agenda to be more evenly distributed between the human and the machine in joint human–machine learning processes, two things need to be considered. Firstly, there is a need to rethink 'failure' and what counts as failure, and secondly the 'fallacy of linear progression' needs to be acknowledged and its position in underpinning much of contemporary self-tracking devices and services needs to be questioned.

Emerging technologies and self-tracking futures

Up to this point we have focused our discussion of technology design and development on the industry contexts where new technologies are developed and commercialized as products. However, new and emerging technologies are also developed in more pure research environments, before they enter markets and are understood within the frameworks of interaction design and user experience, as well as the organized narratives of groups such as Quantified Self. To examine this further we reflect on how the contingent circumstances of science and engineering research, combined with the skill of world-leading engineers, make it possible to imagine new self-tracking futures. To do this we follow the trajectory of an ingestible gas-sensing capsule (Figure 6.3), which has been developed as a new medical technology but also has implications and potential for the future of self-tracking. In 2018 Sarah interviewed the engineer Kourosh Kalantar-Zadeh about the research and development of the capsule, which he and his research team had spent eight years developing in a university research environment (see also Pink forthcoming). Their work is of particular interest for our consideration of self-tracking and personal data futures, since, as described in their published work, 'in contrast to wearable sensors, which are mostly limited to contact with the skin, ingestible sensors can be immersed in the gut, an environment in which the concentrations of chemicals exchanged by our body are high', and this is important, they write, since 'being able to accurately measure the gastrointestinal gases should provide unique insight into the functionality of microbiota, and may enable the development of new diagnostic, therapeutic and monitoring procedures' (Kalantar-Zadeh et al. 2018: 79). The capsule uses sensors to identify and measure gases in the gut, and creates digital data which can be used to detect and potentially

Figure 6.3 The packaged capsule (above) and the open capsule (below), showing the electronic circuit, sensors, packaged batteries and coil antennae. Photo supplied by Kourosh Kalantar-Zadeh.

prevent medical conditions related to gastrointestinal disorders as well as for post-intervention monitoring of the success of medical procedures. The data can be sent directly to a smartphone or other device. It is acknowledged as a major advance in interdisciplinary medical and engineering research, has won numerous international awards and has been widely reported globally across science, technology and popular media channels. This is a highly significant emerging technology for its medical applications, it is considerably more accurate than the conventional alternative of breath testing (Berean et al. 2018), which, as Kourosh described in the interview, had been the objective of the project when it was initially conceived. However, as discussed below, its implications could be far more wide-ranging.

From a social sciences perspective emerging technologies can be thought of as having various characteristics. They tend to be 'constituted as a category of thing in influential public, policy and industry narratives and news media', usually within a narrative of technological innovation and for human good. For example, the *MIT Technology Review* comments of its ten breakthrough technologies for 2018, 'some of our picks haven't yet reached widespread use, while others may be on the cusp of becoming commercially available. What we're really looking for is a technology, or perhaps even a collection of technologies, that will have a profound effect on our lives' (The Editors 2018). *Scientific American* similarly describes their top ten emerging technologies for 2018 in that 'They had to be potentially disruptive, able to alter industries or established ways of doing things. And they had to be in relatively early stages of development – not yet in widespread use but being studied by many groups, generating excitement among experts, attracting increasing investment and, ideally, being developed by more than one company' (DiChristina and Meyerson 2018). In these visions, emerging technologies are set to change the way people experience the world, in ways that will improve our lives.

As discussed elsewhere (Pink forthcoming), Kourosh told Sarah that the capsule had likewise been predicted to have a series of future impacts, including a market of $20 billion for diagnostic uses and an additional market for prevention and monitoring, through its use in place of endoscopy, as a less invasive procedure. What is of most interest here is Kourosh's vision of the future for other future markets for the capsule that were not covered in their scientific publications. He pointed out that the capsule could be taken simply in ways that do not disrupt the users' life and that it moreover 'gives information about the simplest thing that we don't even talk about in any of the papers'. He went on to describe how many illnesses, viruses such as a cold and stress, create changes in the gut, which could be represented by fluctuations in the data from the capsule. In his own experience, he described how 'it happened to me, I had a capsule one day and I became stressed, we had a fluctuation, very very strange ones and I never understood it because we don't know what it is, we even don't know what we are measuring'. For Kourosh this offered a future possibility to create new understanding, if as he put it 'You can imagine, people go and start doing this in millions and the meaning of this data comes out.' In this sense the capsule could be seen as emerging as a personal technology, that people would be able to use to learn about their own bodies. Sarah asked him: 'Would you see it as being available to anybody to use themselves by themselves?'

> *Kourosh:* It can emerge as something that gives information not only about all these things about health but, which is relevant to health, about food, so there's the biggest market on the planet. I think it's bigger than this,

individualized food, diet, prevention ... using diet, to understand the effect of diet, so it's. How many of TV shows are about food ... How we can tell is to have a tool inside our gut to show the reaction to the food to the diet, and then we understand if that is the right kind of diet for us or not. So that's the biggest kind of market, we are talking about trillions of dollars, instead of just 20, 30, 40 millions ...

It's like googling yourself all the time, you are addicted for instance all the time to googling, you want to know information about the simplest thing nowadays and you have the mobile phone, somebody says something the first thing you go and you just find out what it is if you don't know. Just imagine if its about you and your body.

Sarah: And that's what people are already trying to do with all the self-tracking technologies. When they're trying to track their sleep and their heart rates.

Kourosh: This can do more, heart rate is just one of part of billions of kind of parameters we can understand about ourselves, this provides, suddenly goes to, you know, several times more information.

As this example shows, imaginaries for the future of self-tracking emerge not only in the projects of the Quantified Self Movement, or through the uses of existing self-trackers, or through visions of the next iterations of existing self-tracking products, but also in the places of research and development of other technologies that similarly offer ways in which to quantify individual bodies. The example of the ingestible capsule invites us to consider how, as such technologies become increasingly developed and accessible to individual users, such understandings of the body from within could become an everyday experience, taking us beyond the ruptures proposed by the idiosyncratic and experimental nature of biohacking, to conceptualize the idea of tracking the self from inside as a possible future ubiquitous and mundane everyday addiction.

Conclusion

In this chapter we have explored how the futures of self-tracking and personal data are conceptualized, articulated and experienced across a set of different domains of use and design. We have argued for a non-predictive approach to understanding the futures of self-tracking and a correspondingly critical approach to the future-focused 'self improvement' narrative. Instead, we suggest that the meaning of everyday self-tracking has a future orientation that is manifested in a more mundane mode of anticipation, located in and sustained by the routines of everyday life and by the interests of users. This understanding is coherent with our learning approach to self-tracking, outlined in the previous chapter; it suggests that much learning and knowing with self-tracking happens within mundane life and that as such they become bound up with everyday modes of anticipation, which might be equally or, in the case of some of our participants, more important to them as using self-tracking and personal data for future planning and projection. We suggest that likewise future emerging self-tracking technologies, whose data may have wider medical and commercial value, are likely to become ubiquitous technologies in equally mundane ways, just as the mirror and the weight scale discussed in Chapter 3 have. They moreover could benefit from recognizing that to become meaningful to future users self-tracking technologies need to be left open to alternative uses, beyond normative goal-oriented self-improvement narratives, and towards the full diversity of human life.

7

Personal Data Futures

We began this book with our own auto-ethnographic experiences and reflections of using self-tracking technologies that at the time of our completing this book, just four years later, have been discontinued. In July 2018, the *Guardian* newspaper reported that

> The Jawbone UP2, first released in 2015, is a wrist-worn fitness tracker. It connects to iOS and Android phones through Bluetooth, and uploads its data to a companion app, also branded UP. But in 2017, after a run of bad financial results, the company liquidated its assets, and earlier this year it disabled the app entirely. (Hern 2018)

This disrupts the temporal connections that, as we have discussed in earlier chapters, users of self-tracking technologies and personal data experience as they move between present, past and future tenses, learning and meaning-making. The *Guardian* went on to describe how:

> That left existing Jawbone Up users unable to carry on using their fitness tracker, sparking hundreds of complaints on social media. But it also pre-emptively broke unsold products, despite the fact that they were still on shelves across the country. (Hern 2018)

As we have shown in the previous chapters, self-tracking technologies and personal data have fast become embedded in our everyday devices and technologies, memories and imaginations, our ways of sensing both our bodies and the environments around us and in how we know and learn. While, as we have discussed, many people do not actively engage with self-tracking apps and devices for extended periods of time, they nevertheless live in a world where self-tracking has become an option to dip in and out of, or something that other people do. Self-tracking and personal data are ubiquitous as an everyday life *possibility*. For the many people whose smartphone health apps track their steps or other activity automatically they float in the background, not necessarily ever checked but accessible if desired or needed. Some of us regularly receive advertisements from companies such as health insurers marketing self-tracking devices as part of their policies or benefits. Self-tracking and personal data are similarly part of our futures; they are part of lives that have not yet been lived out, in ways that are not yet determined and that people will play an essential role in shaping. While digital self-tracking and personal data have a relatively short history, compared with that of the mirror or the weight scale, they are no longer a new phenomenon. Their short history is becoming dotted with breakages such as that of Jawbone as well as the 2016 voluntary dissolution of the company that made Narrative Clip, which we discussed in Chapter 6, which was reported in the tech industry media (Heater 2016). Breakage is also part of the experience of everyday users whose data becomes disrupted, either when their technologies are discontinued or their apps do not update, or when their own technologies break (Pink et al. 2018). Therefore, as we have argued throughout this book, self-tracking is messy, its future is likely to be just as messy. However, as famously pointed out by the sociologist John Law (2004), making sense in such mess is precisely what social scientists are good at. Bringing together these sense-making skills of the social sciences with approaches from design and pedagogy offers us a way not simply to reflect on what has happened during this short history of self-tracking, but also to propose what might be the way ahead.

In this concluding chapter we draw together the findings presented earlier in this book to argue that the future of self-tracking and personal data will benefit from the building of new relationships between the social sciences, design, industry and users. As we have shown, self-tracking and personal data are often designed for imagined users who do not personify the ways of being human that has been evidenced by both our own ethnographic research and the corresponding anthropological, sociological and pedagogical theory which has been developed by ourselves and others. We argue that there are many possible beneficial uses of self-tracking technologies for change-making across applied research fields such as health, education and safety, but that these will be better realized if the ways that people experience, engage with and imagine their lives with personal data are attended to.

As is evidenced in the discussion of Jawbone UP above, some self-tracking technologies are abruptly becoming obsolete, leaving their users' data and devices 'broken'. Moreover, as we outlined in Chapter 6, new technologies for tracking further aspects of the self are emerging, even if not yet available in our markets. The technological, political and everyday environments in which self-tracking technologies and personal data are used even since our research commenced in 2015 are fast changing; during the course of our research emerging automated and intelligent technologies have become increasingly prominent to the point where we are now confronting what is often seen as a new age of automation. This means that, while our work has offered a baseline of empirical knowledge, and a set of principles concerning how people use, learn, know and imagine futures with self-tracking and personal data, the next generation of research about self-tracking and personal data needs to add to this knowledge and use the principles it has developed to guide how we take on new questions.

This new context is continually emerging. We do not pretend to be able to predict how it will play out and do not recommend solutions to the problems it is purported to bring. Instead we end with a call to approach this situation differently, that is, through a design anthropological agenda that is sensitive to and seeks to disrupt the very societal structures that frame what has been called a 'solutionism' paradigm (Morozov 2013), whereby technologically driven societal change is proposed to solve the problems seen to face people, markets and governance. While this approach still pervades the dominant modes of understanding the ways that emerging technologies will impact on society, it is likely that the technologically driven models that assume that self-tracking technologies and personal data will change human behaviour will persist. Such approaches assume a separation between the user of a technology, who is impacted on, on the one hand, and on the other the designer of a technology who creates the means through which this impact can come about, and the modes of governance or models of business that wish these changes to happen and to those ends disseminate technologies to users. The fundamental problem with this model is that, as we have consistently shown throughout this book, people do not always do what is expected of them with technologies, their uses of them are contingent, personalized and need to have meaning within the context of the mess of everyday life. This model also fails to recognize the power of cultural and historical continuity, and the way in which new routines – and understandings of the potentials of new technologies – are always building upon older embodied routines and understandings of what technology can achieve. This key point is applicable both to the now past scenarios that we have investigated with research participants in their everyday lives as well as to the future, and as yet unknown, scenarios in which they will continue to learn, know and make meanings with such technologies, perhaps delivered in different forms.

Research should never simply be undertaken to provide an analysis for what has happened in the past. Instead, there is an ongoing need to build research and use our existing work to present new agendas for researching in an environment where technology and business are rapidly changing. As researchers engaged in this field we therefore invite our readers to use these principles as a way to reflect on a three questions that we suggest need to inform any future developments in self-tracking and personal data research and design:

- How will people experience, engage and improvise with self-tracking and personal data as artificial intelligence (AI) and automated decision-making (ADM) are increasingly implicated in their representational modes of interaction with users and their management?
- What are the ethics and responsibilities of our self-tracking and personal data futures? What human rights and regulatory frameworks need to be put in place? And how can these be secured?
- What new models and practices of user-designer roles and relationships are emerging in the production, shaping and use of self-tracking and personal data, as new digital economies are coming about?

While the empirical findings of our work form a background to understanding the context from which these possible futures may emerge, the other contribution of our work is to offer a way forward to begin to understand such emerging phenomena and how they will become part of individual lives and societies. This, we propose, needs to be an interdisciplinary approach, that attends to a particular set of concepts:

Time: The past, present and future of self-tracking are set within a context that includes politics, markets and ideologies which shape the ways in which the impact of these technologies in society is publicly and commercially narrated. Simultaneously self-tracking and personal data are part of the ways that people experience the past, present and future of their everyday lives. They are entangled with personal and idiosyncratic, although socially and culturally specific, modes of remembering and anticipating. *To understand self-tracking and personal data as continuously emerging phenomena, we need to take a processual approach to the world, which understands them as part of the world, changing in and with it rather than as something that will impact on people and society as if separate from them.*

Space: Self-tracking and personal data have now become part of the ways our everyday environments are shaped. They can be regarded as spatial technologies in the sense that they participate in how the digital, material and sensory embodied elements of our worlds come together. Our experience of walking through the city while self-tracking using a smartphone is the experience of moving through and documenting our trail in an environment that is at once digital and physical/material. Likewise, as we move through such space, we contribute to its digital composition as our own bodies and activities are rendered into data, and become part of the way that urban space and activity are datafied. *To understand self-tracking and personal data we need to account for how they are part of this continually configuring digital–material environment, which we are likewise part of and contribute to the making of.*

Learning and *Knowing*: Self-tracking and personal data, historically, in the present and as they are imagined into futures, involve learning and knowing the self and body in a range of ways. On the one hand through representational media, such as the mirror image, the dial or figures of the weight scale, and the visualizations of wearables and apps. On the other they are entangled with the sensory and embodied knowing that we do not often verbalize. These sensory ways of knowing are, however, fundamental to the way we learn and feel about such technologies; if we feel comfortable, familiar and 'right' with them, or if we feel anxious or uncertain. We moreover learn and know through self-tracking continually and incrementally, and we do so as part of the wider processes through which these technologies become part of markets and policies. Yet, simultaneously, as we have shown in this book, the ways that the people who constitute the markets for self-tracking technologies use them are not always what is expected by their designers. *Therefore we need to understand such technologies and the possibilities they offer us as also being shaped equally by their users as by their designers.*

Imagining: In this book we have shown how self-tracking technologies and personal data and their impacts are imagined in different and sometimes contesting ways. These differences occur between different academic and applied research disciplines, between users and designers, as well as there being a range of views related to industry and policy perspectives. Each of these different perspectives likewise has a different mode of anticipating the future and correspondingly different future imaginaries for self-tracking. These approaches also have a political aspect to them, as we have demonstrated 'self-improvement' approaches to self-tracking pertain to a predictive futures logic and characterize the neoliberal urge to place responsibility for change on the individual, through 'behaviour change' strategies. In contrast, the approach that we call for distributes responsibility, between users and designers, and other stakeholders. It does not expect users of self-tracking and personal data to follow a directed path of self-improvement towards a better self which is defined with the parameters of the self-tracking app algorithm. *Instead, our approach calls for a particular acknowledgement of the power relations in which self-tracking is embedded. While we recognize the authority of the discourses and politics that surround the use of technology in everyday life, we argue that more emphasis and understanding is needed regarding how people will 'fiddle' with the technologies and apps, how they will improvise with them and how they will use them in ways that are meaningful in their lives. It is these meanings that we wish to see nurtured in a future generation of design for self-tracking and personal data.*

In sum, a new way of thinking about self-tracking and personal data is needed as we move into the 2020s. We hope readers of this book will join us in seeking to shape this as an ethical, responsible and hopeful future.

Notes

Acknowledgements

1   The book was funded through the project 'Sensing Shaping Sharing: Imagining the Body in a Mediatized World' (P14-0367:1).

Chapter 3

1   *Oxford English Dictionary*, s.v. 'datum, n.', OED Online. https://www-oed-com.proxy.mau.se/view/Entry/47434 (accessed 14 July 2019).

2   For an example of this advertisement, see '"Uplift" Changes Brassieres (Part 2): Late 1920's Brassieres', 2016.

3   Information concerning Skokloster and its contents have been derived through interviews and tours Lizette Gradén and Tom O'Dell conducted with curators and personnel at Skokloster. Further information about the painting of Wrangel discussed here can be found in the museum's database, see Livrustkammaren Och Skokloster Slott Med Stiftelsen Hallwylska Museet n.d.-a, n.d.-b.

4   For further information about the Skokloster museum collection, see Livrustkammaren Och Skokloster Slott Med Stiftelsen Hallwylska Museet n.d.-b.

Bibliography

Adams, C. and T.L. Thompson (2016), *Researching a Posthuman World: Interviews with Digital Objects*, London: Palgrave.

Adams, V., M. Murphy and A.E. Clarke (2009), 'Anticipation: Technoscience, Life, Affect, Temporality', *Subjectivity*, 28 (1): 246–265.

Ajana, B., ed. (2018), *Metric Culture: Ontologies of Self-Tracking Practices*, Bingley: Emerald Publishing.

Akama, Y., S. Pink and S. Sumartojo (2018), *Uncertainty and Possibility*, London: Bloomsbury.

Ambjörnsson, R. (2016), 'Så lärde sig människan att se världen på nytt under 1600-talet', *Dagens Nyheter*, 20 March 2016: 38.

Anusas, M. and R. Harkness (2016), 'Different Presents in the Making', in R.C. Smith, K.T. Vangkilde, M.G. Kjærsgaard, T. Otto, J. Halse and T. Binder (eds), *Design Anthropological Futures*, 55–70, London: Bloomsbury Academic.

Apple (2019), 'A Bold Way to Look at Your Health'. Available online: https://www.apple.com/ios/health/ (accessed 28 January 2019).

Apple Developer (2019), 'HealthKit'. Available online: https://developer.apple.com/healthkit/ (accessed 16 January 2019).

ASCIIwwdc (2014), 'Designing Accessories for iOS and OS X'. Available online: https://asciiwwdc.com/2014/sessions/701 (accessed 28 January 2019).

Beer, D. (2016), *Metric Power*, London: Palgrave Macmillan.

Bennett, J. (2010), *Vibrant Matter: A Political Ecology of Things*, Durham, NC: Duke University Press.

Berdugo, L. and M.V. Nicely (2019), 'A New Quantified Self: Embodied Pedagogy and Artistic Practice', *International Journal of Performance Arts and Digital Media*. doi: 10.1080/14794713.2019.1569348.

Berean K.J., et al. (2018), 'The Safety and Sensitivity of a Telemetric Capsule to Monitor Gastrointestinal Hydrogen Production In Vivo in Healthy Subjects: A Pilot Trial Comparison to Concurrent Breath Analysis', *Alimentary Pharmacology and Therapeutics*, 48 (6): 646–654. doi: 10.1111/apt.14923.

Berg, M. (2017), 'Making Sense with Sensors: Self-tracking and the Temporalities of Wellbeing', *Digital Health*, 3: 1–11.

Berg, M. and V. Fors (2017), 'Workshops as Nodes of Knowledge Co-production: Beyond Ideas of Automagical Synergies', in S. Pink, V. Fors and T. O'Dell (eds),

Theoretical Scholarship and Applied Practice, 53–72, New York: Berghahn Books.

Berg, M., V. Fors and J. Eriksson (2016), 'Cooking for Perfection: Transhumanism and the Mysteries of Kitchen Mastery', *Confero*, 4 (2): 111–135.

Bessire, L. and D. Bond (2014), 'Ontological Anthropology and the Deferral of Critique', *American Ethnologist*, 41 (3): 440–456.

Biohacker Summit (2015), 'Biohacker Summir – Panel: Future of Wearables for Health & Wellness' [video], YouTube, uploaded 25 February 2016. Available online: https://www.youtube.com/watch?v=juSm_kCQ2MM (accessed 12 March 2017).

Boellstorff, T. (2013), 'Making Big Data, in Theory', *First Monday*, 18 (10). doi: 10.5210/fm.v18i10.4869.

Boström, H. (1975), 'Ett tyrolskåp på Skokloster', in *Konsthistorisk tidskrift/Journal of Art History*, 44 (1–2): 1–14.

Bowker, G.C. (2005), *Memory Practices in the Sciences*, Cambridge, MA: MIT Press.

Boyd, D. and K. Crawford (2012), 'Critical Questions for Big Data: Provocations for a Cultural, Technological, and Scholarly Phenomenon', *Information, Communication & Society*, 15 (5): 662–679. doi: 10.1080/1369118X.2012.678878.

Boztepe, S. and M. Berg (forthcoming), 'Connected Eating: Servitising the Human Body through Digital Food Technologies', in D. Lupton and Z. Feldman (eds), *Digital Food Cultures*, London: Routledge.

Brogård Kristensen, D. and M. Ruckenstein (2018), 'Co-evolving with Self-tracking Technologies', *New Media & Society*, 20 (10): 3624–3640. doi: 10.1177/1461444818755650.

'The Buyer's Guide: Jawbone Up24' (n.d.), *Engadget*, 16 April 2015. Available online: https://www.engadget.com/products/jawbone/up24/user-scores/ (accessed 7 July 2019).

Carpenter, K. (2003), 'A Short History of Nutritional Science: Part 1 (1785–1885)', *Journal of Nutrition*, 133 (3): 638–645.

Chang, H., F.W. Ngunjiri and K.-A.C. Hernandez (2013), *Collaborative Autoethnography*, Walnut Creek, CA: Left Coast Press.

Cheney-Lippold, J. (2011), 'A New Algorithmic Identity: Soft Biopolitics and the Modulation of Control', *Theory, Culture & Society*, 28 (6): 164–181.

Choe, E.K., N.B. Lee, B. Lee, W. Pratt and J.A. Kientz (2014), 'Understanding Quantified-Selfers' Practices in Collecting and Exploring Personal Data', *CHI 2014, Proceedings of the SIGCHI Conference on Human Factors in Computing Systems*, 1143–1152, New York: ACM. doi: 10.1145/2556288.2557372.

Chun, W.H.K. (2016), *Updating to Remain the Same. Habitual New Media*, Boston: MIT Press.

Clarke, A. (2017), *Design Anthropology Object Cultures in Transition*, London: Bloomsbury.

Clifford, J. and G. Marcus, eds (1986), *Writing Culture: the Poetics and Politics of Ethnography*, Berkeley: University of California Press.

Couldry, N. (2012), *Media, Society, World: Social Theory and Digital Media Practice*, Cambridge: Polity Press.

Crary, J. (1992), *Techniques of the Observer: On Vision and Modernity in the Nineteenth Century*, Cambridge, MA: MIT Press.

Crawford, K., J. Lingel and T. Karppi (2015), 'Our Metrics, Our Selves: A Hundred Years of Self-Tracking from the Weight Scale to the Wrist Wearable Device', *European Journal of Cultural Studies*, 18 (4–5): 479–496.

Crossley, N. (2001), *The Social Body: Habit, Identity and Desire*, London: Sage.

Cukier, K. and V. Mayer-Schoenberger (2013), 'The Rise of Big Data How It's Changing the Way We Think About the World', *Foreign Affairs*, 92 (3): 13.

Dancy, C. (n.d.), 'About'. Available online: http://www.chrisdancy.com/about (accessed 7 July 2019).

Delfanti, A. (2013), *Biohackers. The Politics of Open Science*, London: Pluto Press.

DiChristina, M. and B.S. Meyerson (2018), 'The Top 10 Emerging Technologies of 2018', *Scientific America*, 14 September 2018. Available online: https://www.scientificamerican.com/article/the-top-10-emerging-technologies-of-2018/ (accessed 8 July 2019).

Donahue, J. (2014), 'Up3: A Deep Dive into Sleep Tracking', [blog] Jawbone. Available online: https://jawbone.com/blog/up3-deep-dive-into-sleep-tracking/ (accessed 31 January 2017).

Dourish, P. (2016), 'Algorithms and Their Others: Algorithmic Culture in Context', *Big Data & Society*, published online 24 August 2016. doi: 10.1177/2053951716665128.

The Editors (2018), '10 Breakthrough Technologies 2018'. *MIT Technology Review*, March/April 2018. Available online: https://www.technologyreview.com/lists/technologies/2018/ (accessed 8 July 2019).

Eg Larsen, J., K. Eskelund, and T. Blomseth Christiansen (2017), 'Active Self-Tracking of Subjective Experience with a One-Button Wearable: A Case Study in Military PTSD', *CHI'17*, 6–11 May 2017, Denver, O.

Endeavour Partners (2014). 'Inside Wearables: How the Science of Human Behavior Change Offers the Secret to Long-Term Engagement'. January. Available online: https://medium.com/@endeavourprtnrs/inside-wearable-how-the-science-of-human-behavior-change-offers-the-secret-to-long-term-engagement-a15b3c7d4cf3 (accessed 15 July 2019).

Epstein, D.A., A. Ping, J. Fogarty, and S.A. Munson (2015), 'A Lived Informatics Model of Personal Informatics', *Proceedings of the UbiComp 2015 International Joint Conference on Pervasive and Ubiquitous Computing*, New York: ACM.

Fabian, J. (1983), *Time and the Other. How Anthropology Makes its Object*, New York: Columbia University Press.

Fors, V. (2013), 'Teenagers' Multisensory Routes for Learning in the Museum: Pedagogical Affordances and Constraints for Dwelling in the Museum', *Senses and Society*, 8 (3): 268–289.

Fors, V. (2015), 'Sensory Experiences of Digital Photo-Sharing—"Mundane Frictions" and Emerging Learning Strategies', *Journal of Aesthetics & Culture*, 7 (1). doi: 10.3402/jac.v7.28237.

Fors, V. and S. Pink (2017), 'Pedagogy as Possibility: Health Interventions as Digital Openness', *Social Sciences*, 6 (2): 59.

Fors, V., B. Bäckström and S. Pink (2013), 'Multisensory Emplaced Learning: Resituating Situated Learning in a Moving World', *Mind, Culture, and Activity*, 20 (2): 170–183. doi: 10.1080/10749039.2012.719991.

Fors, V., M. Berg and S. Pink (2016), 'Capturing the Ordinary: Imagining the User in Designing Automatic Photographic Lifelogging Technologies', in S. Selke (ed.), *Lifelogging: Digital Self-tracking and Lifelogging – Between Disruptive Technology and Cultural Transformation*, 111–128, Wiesbaden: Springer.

Fotopoulou, A. and K. O'Riordan (2017), 'Training to Self-Care: Fitness Tracking, Biopedagogy and the Healthy Consumer', *Health Sociology Review*, 26: 54–68.

Futuresource Consulting (2018), 'Futuresource Wearable Technology Market Track – Worldwide Q1 18', 1 June 2018. Available online: https://www.futuresource-consulting.com/reports/posts/2018/june/futuresource-wearable-technology-market-track-worldwide-q1-18/?locale=en (accessed 7 July 2019).

Gehl, R.W. (2014), *Reverse Engineering Social Media: Software, Culture, and Political Economy in New Media Capitalism*, Philadelphia, PA: Temple University Press.

Gibson, J. (1979), *The Ecological Approach to Visual Perception*, New York: Houghton Mifflin.

Gillespie, T. (2014), 'The Relevance of Algorithms', in T. Gillespie, P.J. Boczkowski and K.A. Foot (eds), *Media Technologies: Essays on Communication, Materiality, and Society*, 167–193, Cambridge, MA: MIT Press.

Giroux, H.A. (2004), 'Public Pedagogy and the Politics of Neo-liberalism: Making the Political More Pedagogical', *Policy Futures in Education*, 2 (3–4): 494–503.

Gitelman, L., ed. (2013), *Raw Data is an Oxymoron*, Cambridge, MA: MIT Press.

Gunn, W. and J. Donovan, eds (2012), *Design and Anthropology*, Farnham: Ashgate.

Gunn, W., T. Otto and R.C. Smith, eds (2013), *Design Anthropology: Theory and Practice*, London: Bloomsbury.

Halse, J. (2013), 'Ethnographies of the Possible', in W. Gunn, T. Otto and R.C. Smith (eds), *Design Anthropology: Theory and Practice*, 180–197, London: Bloomsbury.

Hansen, M. (2014), *Feed-Forward: On the Future of Twenty-First-Century Media*. Chicago: University of Chicago Press.

Hargrove, J. (2006), 'History of the Calorie in Nutrition', *Journal of Nutrition*, 136 (12): 2957–2961.

Heater, B. (2016), 'The Narrative Clip Lifelogging Camera Is No More', *TechCrunch*, 28 September 2016. Available online: https://techcrunch.com/2016/09/28/narrative/ (accessed 8 July 2019).

Hern, A. (2018), 'Defunct Jawbone Fitness Trackers Kept Selling after App Closure, says Which', *The Guardian*, 5 July 2018. Available online: https://www.theguardian.com/technology/2018/jul/05/defunct-jawbone-fitness-trackers-kept-selling-after-app-closure-says-which (accessed 8 July 2019).

Hjorth, L. and S. Pink (2014), 'New Visualities and the Digital Wayfarer: Reconceptualizing Camera Phone Photography and Locative Media', *Mobile Media and Communication* 2 (1): 40–57.

Hodkinson, P., G. Biesta and D. James (2008), 'Understanding Learning Culturally: Overcoming the Dualism Between Social and Individual Views of Learning', *Vocations and Learning Volume*, 1 (1): 27–47. doi: 10.1007/s12186-007-9001-y.

Howes, D. (2005), *Empire of the Senses: The Sensual Culture Reader*, Oxford: Berg.

Humphreys, L. (2018), *The Qualified Self: Social Media & the Accounting of Everyday Life*, Cambridge, MA: MIT Press.

Iliadis, A. and F. Russo (2016), 'Critical Data Studies: An Introduction', *Big Data & Society*, published online 17 October 2016. doi: 10.1177/2053951716674238.

Ingold, T. (2000), *The Perception of the Environment: Essays on Livelihood, Dwelling and Skill*, London: Routledge.

Ingold, T. (2012), 'Introduction: The Perception of the User–Producer', in W. Gunn and J. Donovan (eds), *Design and Anthropology*, 19–33, Farnham: Ashgate.

Ingold, T. (2013), *Making: Anthropology, Archeology, Art and Architecture*, Oxford: Routledge.

Ingold, T. and E. Hallam (2007), 'Creativity and Cultural Improvisation: An Introduction', in T. Ingold and E. Hallam (eds), *Creativity and Cultural Improvisation*, 1–24, Berg: Oxford.

Irving, A. (2017), 'The Art of Turning Left and Right', in J. Salazar, S. Pink, A. Irving and J. Sjoberg (eds), *Anthropologies and Futures*, 23–42, London: Bloomsbury.

Jackson, S.J. (2014), 'Rethinking Repair', in T. Gillespie, P. Boczkowski and K. Foot (eds), *Media Technologies: Essays on Communication, Materiality and Society*, 221–239, Cambridge, MA: MIT Press.

Kalantar-Zadeh, K., et al. (2018), 'A Human Pilot Trial of Ingestible Electronic Capsules Capable of Sensing Different Gases in the Gut', *Nature Electronics*, 1: 79–87.

Kersten-van Dijk, E.T., J.H.D.M. Westerink, F. Beute and W.A. IJsselsteijn (2017), 'Personal Informatics, Self-Insight, and Behavior Change: A Critical Review of Current Literature', *Human–Computer Interaction*, 32 (5–6): 268–296. doi: 10.1080/07370024.2016.1276456.

Kickstarter (2012), 'Memoto Lifelogging Camera – Presented by Narrative (2012)'. Available online: https://www.kickstarter.com/projects/martinkallstrom/memoto-lifelogging-camera (accessed 19 December 2018).

Kim, J. (2014), 'Analysis of Health Consumers' Behavior Using Self-tracker for Activity, Sleep, and Diet', *Telemedicine Journal and E-Health*, 20 (6): 552–558.

Kitchin, R. (2014), 'Big Data, New Epistemologies and Paradigm Shifts', *Big Data & Society*, 1 (1). doi: 10.1177/2053951714528481.

Knutsson, J. (1987), 'Mirrors in a Baroque Environment', in *Mirrors at Skokloster Castle: The Exhibition Catalogue for 'For Delight and Utility – Mirrors in a Baroque Environment'*, Skokloster Studies, (21) 6–28, Skokloster Castle Museum: Stockholm.

Kwong, K. (2015), 'A Smart Coach By Your Side', [blog] Jawbone. Available online: https://jawbone.com/blog/smart-coach-side/ (accessed 31 January 2017).

Lave, J. and E. Wenger (1991), *Situated Learning. Legitimate Peripheral Participation*, Cambridge: University of Cambridge Press.

Law, J. (2004), *After Method: Mess in Social Science Research,* International Library of Sociology, London: Routledge.

Li, I., A.K.A. Dey and J. Forlizzi (2010), 'A Stage-Based Model of Personal Informatics Systems', *CHI 2010, Proceedings of the SIGCHI Conference on Human Factors in Computing Systems*, 557–566, New York: ACM. doi: 10.1145/1753326.1753409.

Li, I., A.K.A. Dey and J. Forlizzi (2011), 'Understanding My Data, Myself: Supporting Self-Reflection with Ubicomp Technologies', *UbiComp 2011, Proceedings of the 13th International Conference on Ubiquitous Computing*, 405–414. doi: 10.1145/2030112.2030166.

Light, B., J. Burgess and S. Duguay (2018), 'The Walkthrough Method: An Approach to the Study of Apps', *New Media & Society*, 20 (3): 881–900. doi: 10.1177/1461444816675438.

Livrustkammaren Och Skoklosters Clott Med Stiftelsen Hallwylska Miseet (n.d.-a), 'Samlingana'. Available online: http://emuseumplus.lsh.se/eMuseumPlus?service=direct/1/ResultLightboxView/result.t1.collection_lightbox.$TspTitleImageLink.link&sp=10&sp=Scollection&sp=SfieldValue&sp=

0&sp=5&sp=3&sp=Slightbox_4x5&sp=0&sp=Sdetail&sp=0&sp=F&sp=T&sp=2 (accessed 7 July 2019).

Livrustkammaren Och Skoklosters Clott Med Stiftelsen Hallwylska Miseet (n.d.-b), 'Valkommen Till Var Databas'. Available online: http://emuseumplus.lsh.se/ eMuseumPlus?service=direct/1/ResultDetailView/result.tab.link&sp=13&sp=Scol lection&sp=SfieldValue&sp=0&sp=3&sp=3&sp=SdetailView&sp=583&sp=Sdetai l&sp=5&sp=T&sp=0&sp=SdetailList&sp=0&sp=SdetailBlockKey&sp=0 (accessed 7 July 2019).

Löfgren, O. and R. Willim, eds (2005), *Magic, Culture, and the New Economy*, Oxford: Berg.

Lomborg, S. and K. Frandsen (2016), 'Self-tracking as Communication', *Information, Communication & Society*, 19 (7): 1015–1027. doi: 10.1080/1369118X.2015.1067710.

Lorimer, H. (2005), 'Cultural Geography: The Busyness of Being "More-Than Representational"', *Progress in Human Geography*, 29 (1): 83–94.

Lupton, D. (2014), 'Self-tracking Cultures: Towards a Sociology of Personal Informatics', *OzCHI '14, Proceedings of the 26th Australian Computer–Human Interaction Conference on Designing Futures: The Future of Design*, 77–86. doi: 10.1145/2686612.2686623.

Lupton, D. (2015), 'Health Promotion in the Digital Era: A Critical Commentary', *Health Promotion International*, 30 (1): 174–183.

Lupton, D. (2016a), *The Quantified Self: A Sociology of Self-Tracking*, Cambridge: Polity Press.

Lupton, D. (2016b), 'Personal Data Practices in the Age of Lively Data', in J. Daniels, K. Gregory and T. McMillan Cottom (eds), *Digital Sociologies*, 335–350, Bristol: Policy Press.

Lupton, D. (2017), *Data Thing-Power: How Do Personal Digital Data Come to Matter?*, SSRN, 7 July 2017. doi: 10.2139/ssrn.2998571.

Lupton, D. (2018), 'Digital Health and Health Care', in G. Scambler (ed.), *Sociology as Applied to Health and Medicine*, 277–290, London: Red Globe Press.

Manovich, L. (2013), *Software Takes Command*, New York: Bloomsbury.

Market Research Future (2019), 'Fitness Tracker Market Research Report – Global Forecast to 2023', May 2019. Available online: https://www.marketresearchfuture. com/reports/fitness-tracker-market-4336 (accessed 8 July 2019).

Markham, A. (2013), 'Undermining "Data": A Critical Examination of a Core Term in Scientific Inquiry', *First Monday*, 18 (10). doi: 10.5210/fm.v18i10.4868.

Melchoir-Bonnet, S. (2001), *The Mirror: A History*, London: Routledge.

Merleau-Ponty, M. (1962), *Phenomenology of Perception*, London: Routledge.

Meyer, M. (2013), 'Domesticating and Democratizing Science: A Geography of Do-It-Yourself Biology', *Journal of Material Culture*, 18 (2): 117–134.

Miller, D., ed. (2001), *Home Possessions*, Oxford: Berg.

Moodmetric (2017), 'Moodmetric: Manage Stress Better'. Available online: http://www.moodmetric.com/ (accessed 11 February 2017).

Moore, P. (2018), *The Quantified Self in Precarity: Work, Technology and What Counts*, Advances in Sociology series, Abingdon: Routledge.

Moores, S. (2012), *Media, Place and Mobility*, Basingstoke: Palgrave Macmillan.

Morgan, J. and S. Pink (2017), 'Researcher Safety? Ethnography in the Interdisciplinary World of Audit Cultures', *Cultural Studies ↔ Critical Methodologies*, 18 (6): 400–409. doi: 10.1177/1532708617745094.

Morozov, E. (2013), *To Save Everything, Click Here: Technology, Solutionism, and the Urge to Fix Problems that Don't Exist*, London: Penguin Books.

Nafus, D. (2014), 'Stuck Data, Dead Data, and Disloyal Data: The Stops and Starts in Shifts', *Distinktion: Journal of Social Theory*, 15 (2): 208–222. doi: 10.1080/1600910X.2014.920266.

Nafus, D. (2016), *Quantified: Biosensing Technologies in Everyday Life*, Cambridge, MA: MIT Press.

Nafus, D. and J. Sherman (2014), 'This One Does Not Go Up to 11: The Quantified Self Movement as an Alternative Big Data', *International Journal of Communication*, 8: 1784–1794.

Narrative (n.d.), 'GetNarrative'. Available online: http://getnarrative.com/ (accessed 8 July 2019).

Neff, G. and D. Nafus (2016), *Self-Tracking*, Cambridge, MA: MIT Press.

O'Dell, T. (2013), 'Mobile Spaces of Affect: A Cultural History of the Future', in T. Kaiserfeld and T. O'Dell (eds), *Legitimizing ESS: Big Science as Collaboration Across Boundaries*, Lund: Nordic Academic Press.

Panchasi, R. (2009), *Future Tense: The Culture of Anticipation in France between the Wars*, Ithaca, NY: Cornell University Press.

Pantzar, M. and M. Ruckenstein (2014)., 'The Heart of Everyday Analytics: Emotional, Material and Practical Extensions in Self-Tracking Market', *Consumption Markets & Culture*, 18 (1): 92–109.

Pantzar, M. and M. Ruckenstein (2017), 'Living the Metrics: Self-Tracking and Situated Objectivity', *Digital Health*, 3: 1–10. doi: 10.1177/2055207617712590.

Pantzar, M., M. Ruckenstein and V. Mustonen (2017), 'Social Rhythms of the Heart', *Health Sociology Review*, 26 (1): 22–37. doi: 10.1080/14461242.2016.1184580.

Pink, S. (2004), *Home Truths*, Oxford: Berg.

Pink, S. (2013), *Doing Visual Ethnography*, London: Sage.

Pink, S. (2015), *Doing Sensory Ethnography*, London: Sage.

Pink, S. (2017), 'Ethics in Changing World: Embracing Uncertainty, Understanding Futures, and Making Responsible Interventions', in S. Pink, V. Fors and T. O'Dell (eds), *Working in the Between: Theoretical Scholarship and Applied Practice*, Oxford: Berghahn.

Pink, S. (forthcoming), 'Digital Futures Anthropology', in H. Geismer and H. Knox (eds), *Digital Anthropology*, London: Bloomsbury.

Pink, S. and Y. Akama and contributors (2015), *Un/Certainty* [iBook]. Available online: http://d-e-futures.com/events/uncertainty-symposium/ (accessed 14 July 2019).

Pink, S. and V. Fors (2017), 'Being in a Mediated World: Self-Tracking and the Mind-Body-Environment', *Cultural Geographies*, 24 (3): 375–388. doi: 10.1177/1474474016684127.

Pink, S. and K. Leder Mackley (2013), 'Saturated and Situated: Rethinking Media in Everyday Life', *Media, Culture and Society*, 35 (6): 677–691.

Pink, S. and J. Morgan (2013), 'Short-Term Ethnography: Intense Routes to Knowing', *Symbolic Interaction*, 36 (3): 351–361.

Pink, S. and J.F. Salazar (2017), 'Anthropologies and Futures: Setting the Agenda', in J. Salazar, S. Pink, A. Irving and J. Sjoberg (eds), *Future Anthropologies*, 3–22, Oxford: Bloomsbury.

Pink, S., V. Fors and M. Berg (2017), 'Digital-Visual and Sensory Methodologies for Researching the Experience of Physical Activity', in M. Silk, H. Thorpe and D. Andrews (eds), *Routledge Handbook of Physical Cultural Studies*, London: Routledge.

Pink, S., V. Fors and M. Glöss (2017), 'Automated Futures and the Mobile Present: In-Car Video Ethnographies', *Ethnography*, 20 (1): 88–107. doi: 10.1177/1466138117735621.

Pink, S., V. Fors and M. Glöss (2018), 'The Contingent Futures of the Mobile Present: Beyond Automation as Innovation', *Mobilities*, 13 (5): 615–631. doi: 10.1080/17450101.2018.1436672.

Pink, S., V. Fors and T. O'Dell (2017), 'Editor's Introduction: Theoretical Scholarship and Applied Practice: Opportunities and Challenges of Working in the In Between', in S. Pink, V. Fors and T. O'Dell (eds), *Working in the Between: Theoretical Scholarship and Applied Practice*, 3–28, Oxford: Berghahn.

Pink, S., H. Horst, J. Postill, L. Hjorth, T. Lewis and J. Tacchi (2016), *Digital Ethnography: Principles and Practice*, London: Sage.

Pink, S., L. Leder Mackley, R. Morosanu, V. Mitchell and T. Bhamra (2017), *Making Homes: Ethnographies and Designs*, Oxford: Bloomsbury.

Pink, S., M. Ruckenstein, R. Willim and M. Duque (2018), 'Broken Data', *Big Data & Society*, published online 11 January 2018. doi: 10.1177/2053951717753228.

Pink, S., S. Sumartojo, D. Lupton and C. Heyes LaBond (2017), 'Empathetic Technologies: Digital Materiality and Video Ethnography', *Visual Studies*, 32 (4): 371–381. doi: 10.1080/1472586X.2017.1396192.

Purpura, S., V. Schwanda, K. Williams, W. Stubler and P. Sengers (2011), 'Fit4Life: The Design of a Persuasive Technology Promoting Healthy Behavior and Ideal Weight', *CHI 2011*, 7–12 May 2011, Vancouver, BC.

Quantified Self (2015), 'Welcome to the New QS Forum!' [forum]. Available online: https://forum.quantifiedself.com/ (accessed 8 July 2019).

Quantified Self Institute (2016), 'What is Quantified Self?'. Available online: http://qsinstitute.com/about/what-is-quantified-self/ (accessed 12 July 2019).

Quantified Self Labs (n.d.), 'QS18: Quantified Self Conference, September 22–23, 2018'. Available online: http://qs18.quantifiedself.com/ (accessed 1 June 2018).

Rich, E. (2017), 'Childhood, Surveillance and mHealth Technologies', in E. Taylor and T. Rooney (eds), *Surveillance Futures: Social and Ethical Implications of New Technologies for Children and Young People*, 132–146, Abingdon: Routledge.

Rich, E. and A. Miah (2014), 'Understanding Digital Health as Public Pedagogy: A Critical Framework', *Societies*, 4 (2): 296–315. doi: 10.3390/soc4020296.

Riggare, S. (n.d.), 'Sara's Self-Tracking'. Available online: http://www.riggare.se/saras-self-tracking/ (accessed 8 July 2019).

Rooksby, J., M. Rost, A. Morrison and M. Chalmers (2014), 'Personal Tracking as Lived Informatics', *CHI'14, Proceedings of the SIGCHI Conference on Human Factors in Computing Systems*, 1163–1172, New York: ACM. doi: 10.1145/2556288.2557039.

Rosenberg, D. (2013), 'Data Before the Fact', in L. Gitelman (ed.), *Raw Data is an Oxymoron*, 15–40. Cambridge, MA: MIT Press.

Ruckenstein, M. (2014), 'Visualized and Interacted Life: Personal Analytics and Engagements with Data Doubles', *Societies*, 4 (1): 68–84. doi: 10.3390/soc4010068.

Ruckenstein, M. (2017), 'Keeping Data Alive: Talking DTC Genetic Testing', *Information, Communication and Society*, 20 (7): 1024–1039.

Ruckenstein, M. and N. Dow Schüll (2017), 'The Datafication of Health', *Annual Review of Anthropology*, 46: 261–278.

Ruckenstein, M. and M. Pantzar (2017), 'Beyond the Quantified Self: Thematic Exploration of a Dataistic Paradigm', *New Media & Society*, 19 (3): 401–418. doi: 10.1177/1461444815609081.

Schäfer, M.T. and K. van Es, eds (2017), *The Datafied Society: Studying Culture through Data*, Amsterdam: Amsterdam University Press.

Schüll, N.D. (2016), 'Data for Life: Wearable Technology and the Design of Self-Care', *BioSocieties*, 11 (3): 317–333. doi: 10.1057/biosoc.2015.47.

Segrè, E. (1980), *From X-Rays to Quarks: Modern Physicists and Their Discoveries*, Berkely: University of California Press.

Seyfried, G., L. Pei and M. Schmidt (2014), 'European Do-It-Yourself (DIY) Biology: Beyond the Hope, Hype and Horror', *Bioessays*, 36 (6): 548–551.

Shove, E. (2010), 'Beyond the ABC: Climate Change Policy and Theories of Social Change', *Environment and Planning A*, 42 (6): 1273–1285.

Simon, L. (2004), *Dark Light: Electricity and Anxiety from the Telegraph to the X-ray*, New York: Harcourt Inc.

Smeddinck, J.D., M. Herrlich, X. Wang, G. Zhang and R. Malaka (2019), 'Work Hard, Play Hard: How Linking Rewards in Games to Prior Exercise Performance Improves Motivation and Exercise Intensity', *Entertainment Computing*, 29: 20–30. doi: 10.1016/j.entcom.2018.10.001.

Smith, R.C. and T. Otto (2016), 'Cultures of the Future: Emergence and Intervention in Design Anthropology', in R.C. Smith, K.T. Vangkilde, M.G. Kjærsgaard, T. Otto, J. Halse and T. Binder (eds), *Design Anthropological Futures*, 19–36, London: Bloomsbury Academic.

Smith, R.C., K.T. Vangkilde, M.G. Kjaersgaard, T. Otto, J. Halse, and T. Binder (2016), *Design Anthropological Futures*, London: Bloomsbury.

Sneath, D., M. Holbraad and M.A. Pedersen (2009), 'Technologies of the Imagination: An Introduction', *Ethnos: Journal of Anthropology*, 74 (1): 5–30.

Snyder, L. (2015), *Eye of the Beholder: Johannes Vermeer, Antoni van Leeuwenhoek and the Reinvention of Seeing*, New York: W.W. Norton & Company.

Star, S.L. (2002), 'Infrastructure and Ethnographic Practice: Working on the Fringes', *Scandinavian Journal of Information Systems*, 14 (2): 107–122.

Starker, S. (1989), *Oracle at the Supermarket: The American Preoccupation with Self-help Books*, New Brunswick, NJ: Transaction Publishers.

Strathern, M., ed. (2000), *Audit Cultures: Anthropological Studies in Accountability*, London: Routledge.

Strengers, Y. (2013), *Smart Energy Technologies in Everyday Life: Smart Utopia?*, New York: Palgrave Macmillan.

Striphas, T. (2015), 'Algorithmic Culture', *European Journal of Cultural Studies*, 18 (4–5): 395–412.

Sturken, M. and D. Thomas (2004), 'Introduction: Technological Visions and the Rhetoric of the New', in M. Sturken, D. Thomas and S.J. Ball-Rokeach (eds), *Technological Visions: The Hopes and Fears That Shape New Technologies*, Philadelphia, PA: Temple University Press.

Suchman, L. (1998), 'Human/Machine Reconsidered', *Cognitive Studies*, 5 (1): 1–13.

Sumartojo, S., S. Pink, D. Lupton and C. Heyes LaBond (2016), 'The Affective Intensities of Datafied Space', *Emotion, Space and Society*, 21: 33–40. doi: 10.1016/j. emospa.2016.10.004.

Swan, M. (2012), 'Health 2050: The Realization of Personalized Medicine through Crowdsourcing, the Quantified Self, and the Participatory Biocitizen', *Journal of Personalized Medicine*, 2 (3): 93–118.

Swiderski, R. (2012), *X-Ray Vision: A Way of Looking*, Boca Raton: Universal Publishers.

Thomas, C. (2014), 'Self-tracking Device? Got it. Tried it. Ditched it', [Blog] *The Ethical Nag*, 3 September 2014. Available online: https://ethicalnag.org/ 2014/09/03/self-tracking/ (accessed 7 July 2019).

Till, C. (2014), 'Exercise as Labour: Quantified Self and the Transformation of Exercise into Labour', *Societies*, 4: 446–462.

Tu, J. (2019), 'From "Care of the Self" to "Entrepreneur of the Self": Reconfiguration of Health Care Responsibilities, Needs, and Rights', in *Health Care Transformation in Contemporary China*, 59–84, Singapore: Springer.

'"Uplift" Changes Brassieres (Part 2): Late 1920's Brassieres' (2016), [blog] *Witness2Fashion*, 1 May 2016. Available online: https://witness2fashion. wordpress.com/tag/lastex-girdles-underwear-1930s-thirties/ (accessed 6 June 2018).

Van Dijck, J. (2014), 'Datafication, Dataism and Dataveillance: Big Data between Scientific Paradigm and Ideology', *Surveillance & Society*, 12 (2): 197–208.

Van Dijck, J. and T. Poell (2016), 'Understanding the Promises and Premises of Online Health Platforms', *Big Data & Society*, 3 (1): 1–11. doi: 10.1177/2053951716654173.

Van Dijck, J., T. Poell and M. de Waal (2018), *The Platform Society: Public Values in a Connective World*, New York: Oxford University Press.

Venho, N. (2015a), 'Can I Benefit of Measuring Emotions at Work?', *Moodmetric*, 15 December 2015. Available online: http://www.moodmetric.com/emotions-at-work/ (accessed 20 February 2017).

Venho, N. (2015b), 'Boys' Poker Night Out', *Moodmetric*, 24 May 2015. Available online: http://www.moodmetric.com/boys-poker-night-out/ (accessed 20 February 2017).

Vinkhuyzen, E. and M. Cefkin (2016), 'Developing Socially Acceptable Autonomous Vehicles', *Ethnographic Praxis in Industry Conference*, 29 August–1 September 2016, Minneapolis, USA, 522–534, Wiley Online Library.

Viseu, A. and L. Suchman (2010), 'Wearable Augmentations: Imaginaries of the Informed Body', in J. Edwards, P. Harvey and P. Wade (eds), *Technologized Images, Technologized Bodies*, 161–184, New York: Berghahn Books.

Wang, J., Y. Wang, C. Wei, N. Yao, A. Yuan, Y. Shan and C. Yuan (2014), 'Smartphone Interventions for Long-Term Health Management of Chronic Diseases: An Integrative Review', *Telemedicine Journal and eHealth*, 20 (6): 570–583.

Wertsch, J. (1998), *Mind as Action*, New York: Oxford University Press.

Whiteside, J.A. and D.R. Wixon (1987), 'Improving Human-Computer Interaction: A Quest for Cognitive Science', in J.M. Carroll (ed.), *Interfacing Thought: Cognitive Aspects of Human-Computer Interaction*, 353–365, Cambridge, MA: Bradford/ MIT Press.

Williamson, B. (2015), 'Algorithmic Skin: Health-Tracking Technologies, Personal Analytics and the Biopedagogies of Digitized Health and Physical Education', *Sport, Education and Society*, 20 (1): 133–151.

Williamson, B. (2016), 'Coding the Biodigital Child: The Biopolitics and Pedagogic Strategies of Educational Data Science', *Culture and Society*, 24 (3): 401–416.

Wright, S. and C. Shore (2015), 'Audit Culture Revisited: Rankings, Ratings, and the Reassembling of Society', *Current Anthropology*, 56 (3): 421–444.

Index

For Product Safety Concerns and Information please contact our EU
representative GPSR@taylorandfrancis.com
Taylor & Francis Verlag GmbH, Kaufingerstraße 24, 80331 München, Germany

www.ingramcontent.com/pod-product-compliance
Ingram Content Group UK Ltd.
Pitfield, Milton Keynes, MK11 3LW, UK
UKHW021438080625
459435UK00011B/298